MW00571126

Heating Systems for Your New Home

Richard Kadulski

Illustrations: Terry Lyster

a Solplan Review Handbook

Published by:

The Drawing-Room Graphic Services Ltd.
P.O. Box 86627, North Vancouver, BC V7L 4L2

Distributed by **Gordon Soules Book Publishers Ltd.** ● 1359 Ambleside Lane, West Vancouver, BC, Canada V7T 2Y9 ● PMB 620, 1916 Pike Place #12, Seattle, WA 98101-1097 US
E-mail: books@gordonsoules.com
Web site: http://www.gordonsoules.com
(604) 922 6588 Fax: (604) 688 5442

Copyright 1998

ISBN 0-920768-09-1

Printed in Canada

Dedicated to the loving memory of John and Hedy Kadulski

Acknowledgements

As any writer will tell you, writing is a solitary endeavour. However, that does not mean that all writing is done in isolation on a desert island. This book is the result of many years of discussions among members of the Technical Committee of the Greater Vancouver Home Builders' Association for the need of consumer information about home heating systems.

After many years of talk, I took up the challenge and started on this endeavour. However, I could not do it all myself. I would like to acknowledge the tremendous support, encouragement, and assistance offered by many individuals. I would like to give a special thank you to Ken Farrish and David Hill who went well beyond the call of duty, providing resource materials, commentary and took an axe to several drafts of the manuscript (even trying to rewrite it all!); to Yvonne Kerr who provided encouragement and critical commentary; to George Pinch and Gary Way who provided technical commentary and reviewed the manuscript; Iris Beisiegel who typed; Terry Lyster who did most of the illustrations; and to Jim Stewart who made an attempt to make the text readable. Also, thanks to the many suppliers and manufacturers who provided resource materials.

Canadian Cataloguing in Publication Data

Kadulski, Richard.
    Heating systems for your new home

    "A solplan review handbook."
    Includes bibliographical references and index.
    ISBN 0-920768-09-1
    1. Dwellings—Heating and ventilation. I. Lyster, Terry. II.
    Drawing-Room Graphic Services. III. Title. IV. Title: Solplan review.
    TH7222.K32 1998   697'.07   C98-910694-2

Contents

1. Introduction

Purpose of heating systems: comfort

We cannot forget that the main reason for a heating system is to provide the comfortable indoor environment we need and enjoy. Essentially, your heating contractor is not selling heating systems but comfort systems.

As a species, we humans have outpaced biological evolution and have become dependent on technology to survive. Without shelter to keep us comfortable, we can survive only in a few areas in the tropics. Unlike animals, our bodies are not able to cope with the climate in most places where we live today. Instead, we have learned to clothe ourselves and to build shelter.

Shelter by itself is not enough - usually it has to be tempered with additional heat during the coldest periods of the year, especially in the harsh Canadian environment.

Long ago our ancestors learned that fire offered comfort. The most primitive heat sources were the open fire in a cave or shelter. Over time, this evolved into fireplaces, at first simple stone pits, then masonry enclosures. In Eastern Europe and Central Asia these evolved into elaborate and efficient masonry stoves capable of heating a sizable space in the most severe of climates. These relied on solid fuels for the fire (firewood, dung pellets, or charcoal).

More recently, heaters have evolved into manufactured stoves capable of burning liquid, gaseous or solid fuels. Today we have a wide range of equipment from which to choose. Until recently, these relied on significant human participation to operate them. Today, most are fully automatic.

The wide range of heating products available today makes heating system selection confusing. "What is the best heating system for my house?" is the most frequent question we're asked. Usually more than one heating system is suitable. Unfortunately, little information is readily available to help homeowners and builders assess what is appropriate.

Many competing products make the marketplace a jungle as salespeople make claims that their particular system is the best one. However, remember that while there are many different ways to make our homes comfortable, the physics behind all heating systems is the same.

Despite the many options available and the fact that each has been used for some time, heating systems are the biggest source of homeowner complaints in new houses. A poorly designed or installed heating system will not provide the expected comfort, and can be aggravating, expensive to operate, even dangerous, and depending on system type, remedying any problems can be expensive.

Heating system selection is more complex than for other elements in the house. Cabinets, flooring or hardware can be changed anytime without major consequence to the usability and performance of the house. In fact, this is done often when we want a change of decor. However, that is not possible for most heating systems as they are designed and installed into the very structure of the house, for the most part permanently.

1. Introduction

The intent of this book is to provide information that you can use to evaluate the options available. Hopefully, after reviewing this book, you will have a better understanding of the different heating system options and will be better able to choose a suitable heating system for your new home.

The focus is on the principles behind heating systems, so that you can better understand how they relate to the products on the market, and how various systems may be affected by house design. You will find few product specific references. Rather, the discussion is on generic-product types. This has been done deliberately. Manufacturers constantly modify their product specifications based on ongoing experience and development of new technologies; specific products are discontinued from time to time; and rarely is there only one manufacturer for a specific heating type product. It is more important for you to be an informed consumer, armed with the questions to ask, to make an informed decision before you start looking for a specific product.

The material in this book is primarily aimed at the new home, simply because that is the time when all options are open. When renovating, there are usually fewer options available as revamping the entire heating system may not be possible or appropriate. However, this book should also be useful for those undertaking major renovations, and where older heating equipment may be due for replacement.

As I hope to make clear, there is no one right answer as to the best or most effective heating system for a given house. Some recommendations may appear biased - but then all decisions we make are biased to some extent. However, our suggestions are also based on our experience over more than 25 years of dealing with a variety of residential heating systems and products.

It is also important to recognize that in most jurisdictions heating systems are not inspected. Even in those areas where they are, the inspection focuses mostly on safety details, not comfort or efficiency of the system. Heating standards generally apply to specific equipment and components, but not to the installed system in a house. In other words, they apply to the parts that make up the heating system, but not how they are joined to work as a whole. This may seem like splitting hairs, but it is a significant distinction to keep in mind.

Although qualified trades are required to do the hookup (i.e., gas lines, electrical, plumbing), even correctly installed components can be incorrect in terms of the overall system design (size, layout, control strategy, etc.). Poor heating systems can be costly to operate and maintain; uncomfortable; drafty; noisy; unsafe; under or oversized. Each of these has a price associated with it - either for comfort, efficiency or both.

2. Your House as a System

The house-is-a-system, greater than the sum of its parts. The indoor air quality of a house can be compromised by poor or malfunctioning heating systems.

Recent trends in construction mean better insulated, more draft-free (or airtight) houses with a designed ventilation system. This construction approach has evolved because of a better understanding of how buildings operate and new construction materials and practices. It provides a more comfortable, cheaper to operate, and more durable house. However, it also means that the old ways of thinking must be updated.

When designing and building a home it is important to understand that the movement of heat, moisture and air are interrelated. Their movement is influenced by how the house is constructed, the mechanical systems in the home, the weather, and the home's occupants. Their interactions can affect the home's indoor conditions. In many cases one element cannot be separated from another because there are compatible and incompatible combinations. That is why we say that a *house-is-a-system*.

The idea of the *house-as-a-system* is important to keep in mind, as it will have an impact on how different heating systems are designed. It is no longer good enough to install equipment without considering its impact on other elements in the house.

A woodburning fireplace or woodstove, and any atmospherically vented gas or oil burning heater (furnace, boiler or hot water tank) can spill their combustion gases into the house if you install a high-power exhaust fan (such as a downdraft cooktop) without providing an adequate amount of make-up air to balance the exhaust air. Cooktop salespeople may not mention that you may have to make other hook-ups, because they are probably not well enough informed or not thinking about it. Or, more likely, because they are unwilling to accept responsibility for the potential interaction and feel that the mention of the added requirements may make the product less saleable. However, you will have an unpleasant surprise the first time you switch on the fan when the fireplace is on, as smoke is sucked into the house. This is the most extreme and visible example of interaction between different elements in the house.

Another common problem area is the dryer placed in the furnace room. When it is running, the dryer exhausts a considerable amount of air out of the house. The make-up air needed to compensate for the exhaust will find its way from any direction, including down the flue of the furnace or water heater, thus sucking flue gases back into the house.

More commonly the flue gases from a gas fired furnace or a hot water tank will be sucked back into the house when the other is working. As these flue gases are generally odourless (but still dangerous) you are often not aware of the problem.

Codes are beginning to recognize the problem of equipment interrelation and are limiting the allowable depressurization that can be tolerated in a house. In new B.C. houses many building inspectors will insist on a

Every cubic foot of air that is exhausted must be replaced (otherwise the house would collapse!). Replacement air will find the easiest way into a house - that often is down a furnace or fireplace flue.

2. Your House as a System

test for backdrafting of the flue gases if there are both spillage susceptible appliances and high capacity kitchen fans. However, there is no such inspection if the fan or cooktop is installed later although the potential problem is still there.

The above examples of the interrelationship between seemingly unrelated appliances are a key to understanding the idea of a *house-as-a-system*.

Healthy House

Heating systems can affect the healthfulness of indoor environments.

Today, homes can be designed and operated in a more healthy and sustainable way. Healthy house practices will improve the indoor environment and reduce occupant exposure to irritating, allergenic and potentially toxic pollutants. Some factors affecting the health of the indoor environment are influenced by heating system selection and installation.

Indoor Air Quality

Indoor air quality is not strictly a heating issue, but heating systems can affect indoor air quality.

Indoor air quality is not strictly a heating issue, unless there is a system failure with the combustion equipment. However, heating systems can affect indoor air quality as some can provide air management systems - such as filters and ventilation, humidification, dehumidification, and air circulation.

Heating systems can have a detrimental impact on the health and safety of the house if poorly designed or maintained. To keep the environment inside our homes healthy, care must be given to the design and installation of the heating systems. Proper venting of combustion products is essential for both safety and good indoor air quality.

Effective ventilation, like a good heating system, can provide comfort and is required to provide good indoor air quality. The type of heating system selected will be a determining factor for the type of ventilation system that will be used. In some heating systems ventilation can be integrated into the heating system.

Ventilation systems are required to exhaust air from the bathroom and kitchen, and provide fresh air to control indoor moisture levels, odours, and carbon dioxide. In chapter 9 we discuss ventilation systems in more detail.

Unvented Gas Appliances

Simply put, unvented appliances are incompatible with Canadian homes.

In the United States, there has been a significant growth in the manufacture and sales of unvented gas appliances. Unvented gas fireplaces are a relatively new product. These have a gas burner and ceramic log but no chimney. All exhaust products, heat and moisture are exhausted into the room where the appliance is located. The cost and convenience of unvented fireplaces make them appealing for existing houses.

2. Your House as a System

Unvented fireplaces are sold with an oxygen depletion sensor, a warning that they should not be used continuously as a heating device, that ventilation be provided, and that they be maintained annually by a professional. However, analysis has shown that gases from unvented gas appliances will create conditions that violate Canadian guidelines for indoor air quality. Simply put, unvented appliances are incompatible with modern, energy efficient Canadian homes.

It must be stressed that unvented gas fireplaces will contribute to significant indoor levels of carbon monoxide (CO), carbon dioxide (CO_2), nitrous oxides (NO_x), and other pollutants. Unvented gas fireplaces will also contribute a significant amount of moisture to the house even if they are properly sized, properly installed and diligently maintained, used for no longer than four hours at a time, and installed in a house with an effective, distributed ventilation system.

Gas cooktops also can contribute these pollutants into a home. That is why they should always be equipped with range hoods vented to the exterior whether the code calls for it or not. However, cooktops are usually on for short periods, unlike the fireplaces that may be turned on for many hours at a time. In addition, stoves burn with a blue flame, which is a complete combustion that produces fewer pollutants. The yellow flame in a fireplace is not a complete combustion of the gas fuel, and it produces carbon monoxide.

I recommend that if you have a combustion appliance of any kind in the house, you install a carbon monoxide (CO) monitor. These are inexpensive (typically less than $120) but they will provide peace of mind against any combustion system malfunction.

Gas cooktops should always be equipped with range hoods vented to the exterior.

3. Heating Fundamentals

*Understanding the concepts by which comfort and heat transfer
are described is important to appreciate the properties of heating
systems and helpful when evaluating alternative systems.*

We often forget that the primary purpose of a heating system is
to provide comfort, and heat is just the measurable way to do it. We often
think all that is needed is to maintain a certain temperature, but it is not
that simple. Individually, we each have a range of conditions, dependent
on several factors, at which we are comfortable. Some of these can be
analysed and measured scientifically. Others are subjective.

Home heating systems are really a solution to a body cooling problem.
Our body burns food to provide energy and this always produces heat, so
the body must be cooled to remain comfortable. Our body temperature
has to be maintained at a constant 97-99°F (36.1 - 37.2°C) so we are
always giving off heat. The proper internal body heat balance is maintained by blood circulation. On average we each produce about 400 Btu/
hr (115 watts) of heat that we must loose to the surrounding environment.

What is Comfort?

Comfort conditions vary from person to person within a narrow
range. Our feeling of comfort is influenced by activity level, clothing,
temperature, air movement, humidity and surrounding surface temperatures. A comfortable environment is one in which these factors are in an
appropriate mix. The mix is complex, as a change in one will affect
another. Understanding the subtlety of these factors goes a long way to
understanding the qualities of different heating systems.

Many combinations of air temperature, surface temperatures, air
movement, and humidity that create comfortable conditions are possible,
but all are interrelated. That is why merely maintaining a set air temperature will not always ensure comfort.

The human body can adapt, in a limited way, to a range of these
variables by adjusting its metabolic rate and by sweating or shivering.
One way our body adjusts to cooler temperatures is by closing the pores
to reduce cooling from evaporation and creating "goose bumps" which
reduce convection heat losses by reducing air movement immediately
next to the skin. The rough skin and standing hairs create resistance to
air motion at the surface.

When it is warm, our body reduces heat production and boosts heat
exchange by increasing its surface area through the relaxation of mus-
cles, perspiration, assumption of a limp posture and spreading limbs.
When it is very hot, our metabolism slows and sweating may occur. Body
heat is used to "boil off" water exuding through the pores of the skin.

Clothing is a form of personal insulation to deal with the variable
climate conditions we encounter. Clothing traps pockets of 'dead air'
creating an insulating layer between the body and the environment,
reducing radiation and convection heat losses from the body.

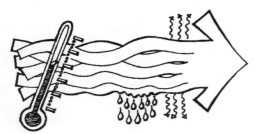

*Many combinations of air temperature,
surface temperatures, air movement, and
humidity create comfortable conditions.*

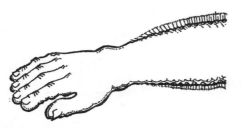

*Goose bumps reduce air movement
immediately next to the skin, thus
reducing convection heat losses.*

3. Heating Fundamentals

It is often thought that comfort conditions are influenced by age, sex, cultural and geographic influences. However, detailed studies in many parts of the world with people of all ages, all races, and all body builds have not discovered any significant differences in optimum conditions. This does not mean that everyone always wants identical conditions. Each of us has their own comfort range that can vary through the day and seasonally. How often have you turned up the thermostat because you feel chilly while your partner follows behind you and turns it down because he or she is too warm?

Human physiology is constantly changing, so we can tolerate a range of conditions. Optimum comfort conditions include some variation of conditions each day and depend on age and activity level. Usually, the younger or the older we are, the less tolerant we are of extremes. As we age, we tend to become less mobile. Blood circulation is not as responsive so our bodies may become more sensitive to cold and require warmer temperatures. This is one reason that retired folks often keep homes warmer and those that can afford it try to spend winter in southern climates.

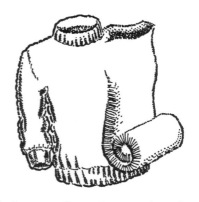

Clothing is a form of personal insulation. It traps pockets of still air creating an insulating layer.

The young active thirtysomething couple may be quite comfortable when the house temperatures are quite cool. A teenager with a very high metabolism might be comfortable with even cooler temperatures (how often do you see teens traipsing along the street in midwinter, with an open jacket, when older folks are bundled up in their down parkas and furs?).

How we were brought up and our expectations of comfort conditions may also be a consideration in establishing a personal comfort range. It was not that long ago that heating systems were very rudimentary and people were accustomed to dressing for the weather. Winter and summer clothes were developed to deal with seasonal temperature variations.

The English or Scots person wearing a thick wool cardigan sweater might be comfortable at 64-66°F (18-19°C), while many Canadians may be unhappy unless the temperature is set at 75-77°F (24-25°C), largely because we do not dress for changeable weather like we used to. In recent years, with the widespread use of central heating, we have become used to walking around the house in bare feet, T-shirts and shorts year round.

Many people commented during the 1998 ice storm in Eastern Canada that there would have been less agony during such a storm at the turn of the century. People then were used to extreme conditions, and dressed for them. Often there was no central heating, but if there was, it was tended manually and did not need electricity to function.

The ASHRAE (the American Society of Heating, Refrigeration and Air Conditioning Engineers) Handbook of Fundamentals, the engineers' "bible," defines thermal comfort as "that condition of mind that expresses satisfaction with the thermal environment." Another way of saying this is that comfort is an absence of discomfort. While this may all seem like much ado about nothing, it underlines that this fundamental idea is too complex to define crisply with measurable numbers.

3. Heating Fundamentals

Standards developed by ASHRAE are based on the set of conditions that will provide comfort conditions satisfactory to 85% of the people. As the environment becomes warmer or cooler an increasing number of persons tend to feel too warm or too cold. That is why some people always seem unhappy in office and commercial environments where conditions are set somewhere near the middle of the comfort zone. They may be persons who find themselves at either end of the average comfort range.

Uniformity of thermal conditions is also important. That is why we want to reduce drafts and have reasonably uniform conditions through the house, otherwise, we would have to move around the house to find comfortable areas. Uniformity of temperatures also means reducing the difference between floor and ceiling, also known as temperature gradients. Rooms with big temperature gradients are often uncomfortable as the coolest temperatures are at the floor, so our ankles feel it immediately. Ankles are one of the more sensitive parts of the body to temperature variations.

Our definitions of thermal comfort do not consider the sound produced, but this also should be considered when choosing heating systems.

Heat Transfer Fundamentals

Before we examine specific heating system types, it is important to review a few fundamentals. These will help us understand the qualities of different heating systems. What we are trying to achieve, in the end, is to have a heating system that will keep us comfortable during the heating season.

When we think heat, images of a fire are always near. The dictionary tells us that the root of the word or idea for heat is from the Greek word to burn.

We must also recognise that heat always flows from a warmer area to a cooler area. Scientists know this as the Third Law of Thermodynamics. A cold area will always gain heat from a warmer area. It does not matter whether it is up, down or sideways. This is a fundamental principle that cannot be forgotten. Many people confuse the effect of rising warm air with the movement of heat. Warm air rises because it is lighter, more buoyant than cooler air. That is the principle of the hot air balloon. It is not the heat that is rising, but the warm air that rises.

A discussion of heat and comfort must also include a review of the way by which heat movement or transfer takes place. From physics we know that there are three means of heat transfer: *conduction, convection,* and *radiation*.

Conduction

Conduction is the flow of heat through matter (solids, liquids or gases) or from objects in contact with each other, always from hot to cold. Conduction heat transfer depends on the temperature difference between the materials and the ability of the materials to transfer heat (its conductivity), and the amount of material.

Heat transfer is always from hot to cold.

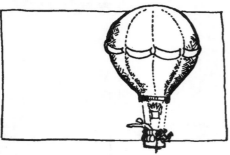

Warm air rises because it is lighter, more buoyant than cooler air. It is the warm air, not the heat that keeps a hot air balloon afloat.

Conduction is not a significant heat transfer mechanism in heating systems.

When two objects touch, heat moves directly from the warmer to the cooler one. Some objects are better conductors than others. Metals and water are good conductors of heat, while air is a poor conductor. Anyone burned by touching a hot iron, or cooled by holding an ice cube is aware of heat flow by conduction.

Conduction is not a significant heat transfer mechanism in heating systems.

Convection

Convection is the movement of heat due to motion in a liquid or gas, such as air, from a warmer to cooler area. When the molecules of a fluid are heated, that portion of the fluid expands and weighs less than the surrounding, cooler portion. The heated portion of the fluid will thus be lighter so it rises, to be displaced by cooler, denser fluid.

Convection currents are very important in heating systems, as convection currents from ducts and heating elements such as baseboards distribute the heat. Forced convection by fans or pumps enhance convection flows, allowing equipment to be more compact.

The human body is more comfortable when most of its heat is shed by convection. Thus, an air temperature lower than body temperature is necessary to allow sufficient body cooling by convection.

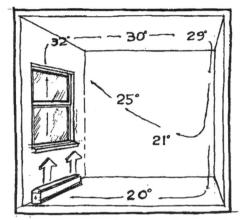

Convection currents are very important in heating systems.

Radiation

Radiation is the direct transfer of energy by electromagnetic waves from an object at a higher temperature to an object at a lower temperature. Heat may radiate through a vacuum (as from the sun to the earth), through air (as from a hot stove to the other side of the room), or through a material such as glass that is transparent to the particular wavelengths involved.

If two objects at different temperatures can "see" each other, they will tend toward the same temperature by radiation. An example is the feeling of cold you may experience when sitting beside a cold window at night when the inside is warm, but the outside is cold.

Radiation does not heat the air as it passes through, but heats any objects that it may strike, such as a human body, floors, furnishings and walls. Examples of radiant heat transfer include: the warmth felt from sitting near a fire, being exposed to the sun, and being heated by radiant floor or ceiling heating systems.

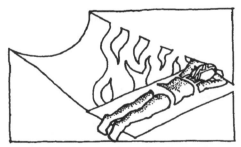

Radiation does not heat the air but heats any objects that it may strike.

Factors Affecting Comfort

Air Temperature

Temperature is a measure of heat intensity. Dry-bulb temperature, usually known as the air temperature, is the temperature taken with a thermometer not in contact with water or influenced by radiation. Wet bulb temperature is measured with a wetted thermometer in rapidly moving air. The relationship between "dry bulb" and "wet bulb" temperatures is used to establish the relative humidity.

3. Heating Fundamentals

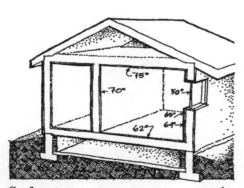

Surface temperatures can vary across the room.

Mean radiant temperature (which describes the average temperature of surfaces surrounding a person in a room) is one of the most important elements affecting comfort. The mean radiant temperature can vary from point to point within a room.

The temperature within a room is usually not even. Often there is a significant variation between the air temperature at the floor and ceiling (known as temperature stratification). The air temperature required for comfort depends on air movement, kind and level of physical activity, type of clothing worn, age and the amount of thermal radiation to or from the room surfaces. People seated in a room may be comfortable at an air temperature of 70°F (21.1°C), but if there are large glass areas the air temperature may have to be raised to 74°F (23.2°C). Where people are physically active (as in a gym) then 50°F (10°C) may be enough. Residential heating systems are normally designed to provide indoor temperatures of 72°F (22.2°C).

Heat transfer from a body to its surroundings happens when the surface of the body is at a higher temperature than its surroundings. That is why surface temperatures of a room have a big impact on comfort. A room has several surfaces, each of which can be at different temperatures, depending on the room's finish and thermal insulation. Windows are usually the coolest surfaces.

Radiant heat transfer is always from hot to cold. It can mean moving through the vacuum of space - as the sun heats the earth through air (without heating the air). The warm human body "sees" cold surfaces, so it will radiate heat to them, thus creating a cooling sensation. Skin responds very quickly to radiant heat. For example, at 50°F (10°C) it may feel warm in the sunshine, as the body responds to the hot sun. However, when a cloud moves in front of the sun, you instantly feel cooler, although the air temperature has not changed.

Mean Radiant Temperature

How much body heat is lost by radiation depends on the surface temperatures in the room. Engineers have developed the concept of *mean radiant temperature* to define surface temperatures. This is one of the most important elements affecting comfort. Mean radiant temperature is an average temperature of surfaces (walls, floor, ceiling, windows) surrounding a person. It is also a measure of the radiant heat exchange between a person and their surroundings. The mean radiant temperature is dependent on the relationship of the surface to the person and can vary from point to point within a room.

The qualities of the surrounding surfaces are also important, as they determine how good a reflector the surfaces are. With a perfect reflector, the radiant energy loss from a person is reflected back, at the same body temperature as the person, and there will be little discomfort. Of course, there is no such thing as a perfect reflector. When there are several surfaces at different temperatures, as is the usual case, the effect of the mean radiant temperature becomes more significant and can contribute to significant discomfort (i.e. cold rooms).

3. Heating Fundamentals

A simple formula has been developed that allows normal comfort level of a room to be calculated by adding the two primary heating components: air temperature and mean radiant temperature (average room surface temperature). The formula is: air temperature (°F) + mean radiant temperature (°F) = 140 (°F).

For example, with a conventional forced warm air heating system we can maintain comfortable conditions at an air temperature of about 72°F (22°C) with a mean radiant temperature of 68°F (72 + 68 = 140). With a radiant heating system, comfort is achieved at 68°F air temperature if the mean radiant temperature is 72°F (68 + 72 = 140). The fact that the air temperature in a room is 68 or 72°F is no guarantee of comfort. A room with a temperature of 67°F (19°C) may feel warmer than a room in which the air temperature is 72°F if the walls, ceiling and floor are warm.

Drapes in front of large picture windows at night can improve comfort by reducing the radiant heat loss, as the surface of the fabric now becomes the radiant surface and the temperature of the fabric is warmer than the cold window surface so we do not lose as much radiant heat.

Heating registers and radiators are typically placed against the outside wall, under windows, to heat the coolest part of the envelope (the windows), thus reducing the radiant heat loss, and also reducing cold convective air currents washing down the wall.

Relative Humidity

Relative humidity is a measure of how much water vapour is in the air compared with the amount that air could hold if it were completely saturated. Relative humidity levels are dependent on air temperature. Very low or very high humidity levels are uncomfortable. The optimum relative humidity is in the 30-60% range. Conditions outside this range are not as healthy as our resistance to viruses drops.

At high humidities and warm temperatures, perspiration that forms on our skin does not evaporate quickly enough, thus reducing heat loss and contributing to overheating and discomfort. In extreme conditions, we feel sweaty (as happens on a hot, humid summer day). At higher humidities the air temperature can be cooler for an equivalent comfort level. If the relative humidity rises much above 60% (especially in the winter), conditions are good for the growth of moulds and mites that are also a health concern.

Very dry conditions (relative humidity of less than 20%) can easily be attained during very cold weather in the winter. When the air is too dry, our skin and mucous membranes dry out (in other words, our body dehydrates). When the relative humidity is too low, the air temperature has to be

A simplified formula for comfort conditions is as follows:

air temp (°F) + mean radiant temp (°F) = 140 °F

Outdoor-Indoor Relative Humidity Conversion

Exterior RH	Indoor Humidity (at indoor temp of 70 °F) for corresponding exterior temperatures								
	-20°F	-10°F	0°F	10°F	20°F	30°F	35°F	40°F	45°F
	-18.8°C	-23.3°C	-17.7°C	-12.2°C	-6.6°C	-1.1°C	+1.6°C	4.4°C	7.2°C
100%	2	4	6	9	17	23	29	36	43
90%	2	3	5	8	15	21	26	31	39
80%	2	3	5	7	13	19	23	27	25
70%	1	2	4	6	11	17	20	24	31
60%	1	2	3	5	9	14	17	21	26
50%	1	1	3	5	8	12	14	18	22

figures in chart are percentages

For example: outdoor air at 0°F and 90% relative humidity when warmed to 70°F will have a relative humidity of 5%.

3. Heating Fundamentals

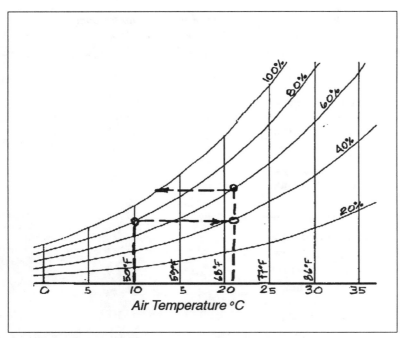

How to use a psychometric chart: Dry bulb temperature is plotted across the bottom, the curves represent relative humidity. As one changes, the other will too. For example, if air at 10 °C (50 °F) and 80% relative humidity is heated to 21 °C (70 °F), the RH drops to 40%.
The 100% RH curve is the point at which condensation will happen. if the air at 21 °C and 60% RH is cooled, at 12.6 °C (55 °F) condensation will take place. This point is referred to as the dew point for that air-vapour mixture.

increased to compensate for the dryness, and humidification of indoor air should be considered. Humidification is generally not required in mild climates, such as coastal regions of BC, any time of the year.

Indoors in winter, relative humidity levels are generally dictated by how much indoor air is exchanged with outdoor air. When the outside air is below freezing there is so little moisture in the air that even when a small amount of outdoor air is brought inside and heated to indoor conditions, the indoor relative humidity is reduced. Even on the mild West Coast, with its high rainfall and 80-90% outdoor relative humidities, air exchange with the interior will reduce indoor relative humidity.

The relationship between humidity and air temperature can be plotted on a psychometric chart. The psychometric chart is used by mechanical designers to predict conditions at which condensation may take place when designing cooling systems and to anticipate and avoid condensation problems. It can tell us when condensation could be a problem in a cool basement in the summer, or on the fresh air intake ducts in winter.

Air Movement

Moving air generates convection heat loss and a cooling sensation.

Moving air generates convection heat loss and a cooling sensation on our skin. Air movement over the skin evaporates moisture (our perspiration) into the air, cooling the body. As moisture evaporates, heat is required. To evaporate sweat, energy is drawn from our body, thus creating a cooling effect. The rate of evaporation (and heat loss) is directly related to the rate of air movement and relative humidity. An example is the "cooling" that we feel when we walk out of a hot shower or when a summer breeze passes over us.

Air flowing past the neck and ankles is critical, as these two areas of exposed skin are sensitive to drafts. Grandma knew this instinctively, when she knitted scarves and wool socks for the family for the winter.

In hot weather a fan is used to stimulate air movement to cool us. When you are seated near a fan, you may feel a cool draft even though the air temperature may be high - in the 77-86°F (25-30°C) range. This is because the high velocity of air sweeping over the body produces a higher than normal rate of convective and evaporative body heat loss.

3. Heating Fundamentals

In the winter, when heating is wanted, too much air movement leads to discomfort. However, because the heat storage capacity of air is small, it takes much air to move even small quantities of heat. At times and at certain points in a room, such as near a forced air register, air movement may be at very high velocities. One reason that forced air heating systems have to circulate hotter air is to ensure that the air movement does not chill us. In a poorly laid out or oversized forced air heating system, large volumes of air movement will create this discomfort. It will feel like unwanted drafts.

Energy Units

There are almost as many terms to express units of heat energy as there are sources of energy. Gigajoules, Btu's, kilowatt-hours, therms and others are all used to express heat energy in one form or another. To add to the confusion, energy is sold in various units of measurements that may have no resemblance to a unit of energy. Natural gas can be sold by volume (cubic metres) or energy units, oil by the litre, propane by volume or weight, electricity by the kilowatt-hour, and wood by the cord (unrelated to species or condition.).

The basic energy unit in the Imperial system is a British thermal unit or Btu. By definition a Btu is the heat required to raise 1 pound of water 1 degree Fahrenheit. An appliance is generally rated in Btu/hr which is the maximum amount of energy that the unit will consume or produce in an hour.

The metric unit of heat energy is the joule, which is a very small unit. One joule equals 0.00095 Btu. 1000 joules (1 kilojoule) is about 5% larger than a Btu (1055 joules = 1 Btu). As the joule is such a small unit, the common metric term is the Gigajoule (GJ) or 1 billion joules, which is about 948,200 Btu.

A kilowatt-hour (kWh) is the energy unit for electricity, which is equal to 1000 watt hours. 1 watt = 1 joule/sec. 1 kWh equals 3413 Btu or 3600 joules.

A 1000 watt electric heater is capable of producing heat at the rate of 3413 Btu/hr. The 3 kW (3000 watt) element in an electric water heater is capable of producing 10,239 Btu/hr, which will heat 100 pounds of water (10 imperial gallons) from 40°F to 140°F in 59 minutes.

It is difficult to compare the various energy types when they are measured in different units. The bottom line you are interested in is what the cost of heating your hour is going to be. That is why we've compared the cost of fuels based on equivalent quantities of energy. The table is on page 34.

4. Calculating Heat Loss

Heating system design must be based on a careful calculation of the home's heat requirements. Understanding the elements that contribute to the heat loss of a house can be used to make decisions about construction details that will reduce heat loss in the first place.

The *design heat loss* of a house is the total amount of heat lost through all the building components on the design day for that location, with an indoor temperature set at 22°C.

It is very important that the design of the heating system for each house be based on calculation. Calculations are necessary for accurate sizing of heating equipment, to avoid over or under sizing heating equipment. They are far more reliable and accurate than contractors' rules of thumb. They can also be used to determine the best place to spend your money for the most cost effective and energy efficient house design. A few jurisdictions now require that heat loss calculations be done for all heating installations.

Efficiency in operation is lost if the heater is oversized. On the coldest night of the year, the heating appliance should be running continuously. It is similar to the notion that you get better gas mileage on the highway than in stop-and-go city traffic. Heating system sizing calculations usually have a safety factors of about 10-20% built into the procedures, so the contractor does not need to add in a large "fudge" factor, as they frequently do.

The most important part of providing thermal comfort rests with the construction of the home itself - the design of the thermal envelope, its insulation levels and quality of construction. The heating system is there to make up the difference for the climate in which we live. It is something we have forgotten in recent years as equipment has become available to make a leaky glass box habitable whether it is built in the high arctic of the Northwest Territories, the cold plains of Saskatchewan, coastal BC, or the Arizona desert. The severity of the climate just makes it more or less expensive to force the comfort conditions into that glass box, with varying degrees of success. In most cases, identical equipment is found in all locations - just the heating capacity is different.

I cannot stress enough: the starting point should be a house design suited to its climate with good insulation levels. Currently, building codes at best have very minimal insulation standards. The minimum that should be used in a new house are the levels set out in the Model National Energy Code for Houses (which has not yet been adopted by any jurisdiction), or even better, the standards required by the R-2000 New Home program.

Heat Loss Calculations

Heat loss calculations take into account the fact that heat is lost mainly by the building shell (the envelope) and air leakage. For the building envelope components, the formula takes into account the area of the building component, the resistance to heat flow (the R-value), and the temperature difference between interior and exterior. The temperature difference is based on the difference between outdoor design temperature and interior design conditions, usually 72°F. The 2½% dry bulb design temperature is used in all calculations. It is based on long term local climatic data that has been established for every community, and is the coldest temperature which has been reached outdoors over 97½% of the recorded time.

Many computerized programs are now available to help in the calculations. Some equipment manufacturers have their own proprietary versions to do these calculations. For zoned systems, the calculation should be done "room-by-room." For central systems, a whole house calculation is enough for sizing the heating unit. However, a room by room analysis is required to ensure proper distribution of heat.

The heat loss calculation is done for each envelope component (walls, ceilings, windows, doors, floors in contact with exterior). Some may have differing insulation levels, so each has to be taken into account. For example, one wall may be 2x6, and another may be 2x4; a vaulted ceiling usually has a lower insulation level than a flat ceiling with attic above.

You should be aware that just because a 2x6 wall can hold an R-20 insulation batt it will not have an insulation value of R-20. The effective insulation value is usually lower, because of the thermal bridging through the framing and studs, plates, lintels and trim materials.

Our example shows how changing the insulation levels and type can have an impact on the overall heat loss of the house, and consequently the energy consumption of the house. It is always worth considering details that reduce the heat load of the house. Better insulated walls and ceilings will not only reduce the heat loss but are also warmer on the inside, thus raising the mean radiant temperature. These contribute to a healthier indoors, as warm surfaces are not likely to experience condensation on the surface, which means less conditions for moulds and fungi to grow.

It is worth considering how important a given component is as part of the total. A component responsible for ⅓ of the heat loss, if upgraded, will have a bigger impact on total heat loss than one that is responsible for only 2%. For example, because ceilings are usually reasonably well insulated, adding more insulation will not always have the same impact as insulating an uninsulated or poorly insulated basement wall. As changes are made, and the insulation levels of specific components are upgraded, the ratio may increase slightly, but it will be a piece of a smaller pie.

Windows

Windows are usually the single largest component of heat loss in a house and merit special attention. In a typical house, 30 to 50% of total heat loss may be by way of the windows. However, windows have undergone many technical developments in recent years.

Today's high performance windows are reliable energy efficient performers. Frame and hardware design are not the only elements for consideration. There is a wide range of glass products on the market. All

As a formula, the heat loss calculation looks like this:

$$HL = (A/R) \times dT$$

HL = heat loss (BTU)
A = surface area of component (e.g. exterior walls)
R = thermal resistance value
dT = temperature difference

Engineers use a U value, which is almost the same as 1/R.

Sample Wall Insulation Values			
Framing	Insulation	Nominal R-value	Actual R-value
2x4 @ 16"o/c	R 12 fibreglass	12	11.56
2x6 @ 16"o/c	R 20 fibreglass	20	16.88
2x6 @ 24"o/c	R 20 fibreglass	20	17.14
2x4 @ 16"o/c	R 12 fibreglass plus R7 exterior insulation	19	18.51

Better insulated walls and ceilings are warmer on the inside, raising the mean radiant temperature. These contribute to a healthier indoors.

In a typical house, 30 to 50% of total heat loss may be by way of the windows.

4. Calculating Heat Loss

Window ratings use formulas to predict the performance of windows under assumed conditions. The Energy Ratings (ER) are intended for comparison purposes using a formula defined in the CSA window standard. Other labelling systems focus on specific features of interest to program sponsors. These include:
BC Hydro's Power Smart program
Canadian Window and Door Manufacturers' Association (CWDMA)
NFRC in the USA

In drafty older houses air leakage can account for half the total house heat loss.

Air leakage is one cause for stained carpet edges, especially noticeable on light coloured carpets.

low emisivity (low-e) coatings do not have the same properties, so be sure to ask your supplier to explain all their options. The lower the U value (the higher the R value) the better the thermal performance. This means there will be less heat loss, less condensation on the windows in winter, and increased comfort.

Windows can be selected to allow sun in or to keep the sun out, so you can choose windows depending on their location on the house for the properties you need. A helpful comparison tool are the energy ratings (also known as ER). The higher the ER number, the better the window is. A typical operable thermally-broken aluminum frame window with clear double glass with aluminum spacers has an ER rating of -50. An operable wood frame window with low-e glass, insulating spacer, and argon gas has an ER rating of -10, while the same unit that is a picture window may have an ER of +2 or better.

Air Leakage (Infiltration) Heat Loss

A house also loses much heat by uncontrolled air leakage through holes and cracks in materials that make up the building envelope, separating the interior from the exterior, and also through controlled ventilation. The leaks can happen where two or more materials are joined. It can be at door and window frames, around electrical outlets, at floor ceiling and wall floor junctions, and around chimneys, electrical panels and duct penetrations to the exterior. In older drafty houses this air leakage can account for as much as half the total house heat loss.

Air leakage compromises comfort, by allowing uncontrolled drafts. It increases the heating bill, and often contributes little toward improving the indoor air quality. The air leakage is greatest when the temperature difference between inside and outside is maximum (as happens in cold winter weather).

An airtight house is a draft-free house, and thus more comfortable. Establishing how airtight the house is difficult unless a test is done, as happens for R-2000 Homes. Based on testing in Canada for the past fifteen years, we know that houses in all parts of the country are increasingly getting more airtight. However, special effort is required when building to ensure that the house is draft-free.

Design Heat Load

The design heat load of a house is determined by adding the heat loss of each component. This provides a figure that tells us how much heat the heating appliance has to supply at this design temperature. The size of the heater should be close to what is calculated.

Our example shows the results for a typical modest two storey house, 1800 square feet plus a basement. We have assumed the house is located in Kamloops, BC (design temperature -25°C). The calculations were derived using the HOT-2000 energy calculation software, and use effective insulation values. (Nominal insulation values are also noted). No special considerations are assumed for optimizing the design for solar gains.

4. Calculating Heat Loss

To show the effect of upgrading various building components, we have assumed the "base case" is the house built to meet the requirements of the BC Building Code. The first upgrade would be if the house were built to meet the standards of the Model National Energy Code for Houses (MNECH), and the third upgrade is what would be required to meet R-2000 standards.

Heat loss for sample house (2 storeys, 1,800 sq.ft. plus basement)

Component	Net Area (sq.ft.)	Base Case			MNECH (Energy Code)			R-2000		
		Construction	Effective R value (nominal R value)	% of total heat loss	Construction	Effective R value (nominal R value)	% of total heat loss	Construction	Effective R value (nominal R value)	% of total heat loss
Ceiling	930.6	attic trusses	39.86 (R40)	2.61	attic trusses	45.06 (R44)	2.50	attic trusses	50.6 (R51)	3.15
Exterior wall	1751.4	2x6 @ 16" c/c, R20 batt insul, siding	15.44 (R20)	15.27	2x6 @ 16" c/c, R22 batt insul, siding	16.72 (R22)	15.11	2x6 @ 16" c/c, R22 batt insul, siding	16.72 (R22)	21.48
Exterior Doors	58.0	metal insulated	6.47 (R12)	1.45	metal insulated	6.47 (R12)	1.55	metal insulated	6.47 (R12)	2.21
Exposed floors	10.7	2x10 @ 16" c/c, R28 batt insul	29.05 (R28)	0.05	2x10 @ 16" c/c, R28 batt insul	29.05 (R28)	0.06	2x10 @ 16" c/c, R28 batt insul	29.05 (R28)	0.08
Windows	289.0	clear double glazed, metal spacers, vinyl frame	1.95 (R2)	23.94	low-e double glazed, metal spacers, vinyl frame	2.53 (R3)	20.1	low-e double glazed, argon fill, insulated spacers, vinyl frame	2.99 (R3)	24.21
Basement walls above grade	377.8	2x6 @ 16" c/c, R20 batt insul	15.99 (R20)	3.52	2x6 @ 16" c/c, R22 batt insul	17.51 (R22)	3.45	2x6 @ 16" c/c, R22 batt insul	17.51 (R22)	4.92
Upper basement wall	275.1	concrete wall, R12 insulation	13.95 (R12)	1.49	concrete wall, R10 insulation	11.36 (R10)	1.91	concrete wall, R20 insulation	17.51 (R20)	3.47
Lower basement wall	522.7	uninsulated concrete wall	1.34 (R0)	12.04	uninsulated concrete wall	1.34 (R0)	12.84	concrete wall, R12 insulation	11.93 (R12)	4.63
Basement floor	873.0	uninsulated concrete floor	1.16 (R0)	6.35	uninsulated concrete floor	1.16 (R0)	6.8	uninsulated concrete floor	1.16 (R0)	12.88
Ventilation (air exchange)	22,367 cu.ft.	"average" air tightness, code minimum ventilation		33.27	code air tightness, minimum ventilation		35.66	R-2000 airtight construction, with heat recovery ventilator		22.97

The results are summarized in the table at right. They show that the capacity of the heating system in an energy efficient house (meeting R-2000 criteria) can be reduced by 25%, and the total energy consumption will be cut by more than half!

The specific numbers will vary from house to house, and city to city, but the general relationship will be the same.

Heat loss comparison for sample house		
Case	Design Heat Loss (BTU/hr)	Estimated annual space heating consumption (kWh)
Base case (present code construction)	56,277	28,655
National Energy Code Standards	52,604	26,220
R-2000	43,636	12,988

5. Basic Components of a Heating System

Heat source, distribution, and controls are the fundamental components of any heating system. The specifics of various heating system types are discussed in chapter 7.

Regardless of the type, all heating systems have three common components: a heat source, a distribution system and controls. Before we get into a detailed look at heating systems, it is worth reviewing these basic elements. When these are not well designed, installed or understood, the system will not do the job it was intended to do.

Heat Source

Fuel type defines the source of the heat energy, not the type of heating system. Fuel selection should be based on local availability, costs, local trade practices, and house design. In most locations several fuel types are available.

The most common fuel sources used today include:

> *Natural Gas*
> *Oil*
> *Electricity*
> *Propane*
> *Wood*
> *Solar*

Every heating system must, by definition, have a source of heat or a "heating appliance." In a forced air heating system it is a furnace, in a hydronic system it may be a boiler or water heater, in electric resistance heating it is the electric heating element that could be in the baseboard, radiant panels or heat pump. Cottages and smaller, older houses are often heated by a wood stove. In a passive solar house, the source of heat is the sun.

We need to consider two points when we look at the heat source: one is the heating appliance, the second is the fuel type.

The heating appliance generates the heat. Many types are available, such as a furnace, boiler, water heater, baseboards, stove, or fireplace. Specific choice may depend on the fuel type chosen. Most appliance types have various fuel options. For example, a furnace or boiler can be fired by any fuel type (electric, gas, oil or even wood).

Many houses take advantage of at least two fuel sources: the fuel used in the principal heating system and solar energy. One may not always think about the sun except for specially designed solar houses. Yet most houses with some south facing windows may get 10 to 25% of the seasonal heat energy required from the free solar energy that enters through south windows. However, most houses cannot take full advantage of the solar energy because their design does not optimize solar gains, or the house does not have adequate thermal storage to absorb and store the heat.

One of the biggest problems is oversized heaters not matched to properly sized distribution systems. They jeopardize comfort, equipment efficiency, health and safety, and can shorten the life span of the heating equipment.

One of the biggest problems is the installation of oversized heating appliance units. Oversized heaters not matched to adequately sized distribution systems jeopardize not only comfort and equipment efficiency, but more importantly health and safety, and can shorten the life span of the heater.

Distribution

The heat generated by the heat source must be distributed. In forced warm air systems, ducts are the distribution system. In a hydronic system, piping is used. In unitary electric systems, radiators/convectors are used. The type of heat distribution is perhaps the most important element that defines the comfort of your heating system.

5. Basic Components of a Heating System

Convection and radiation are the main ways heat is distributed in a home. Forced warm air heating distributes all heat by convection, radiant systems (floor or ceiling) distribute it by radiation. Modern shielded baseboards are convection only heaters (unlike the old fashioned cast iron radiators which were true combination radiators and convection heaters).

Convection is the transfer of heat energy due to motion in air. A baseboard heater (known to the industry as a convector) warms the air by heating the air immediately surrounding the hot fins. The warmed air flows up and around the room. The volume and speed of air flow is slow, so that it is not usually perceptible.

Radiation is the direct transfer of energy by electromagnetic waves from a hotter object to an object at a cooler temperature. In radiant heating systems, the panel heated (ceiling or floor) radiates the heat to the colder surfaces of the room (walls, furniture, people). When you walk on a radiant heated floor you also get some heat by conduction. Baseboards also radiate some of their heat.

Radiant heated floors also have significant convection component, as air near the floor is warmed and rises.

Controls

Every heating system has to control how much heat is supplied to those areas where we want it. It can be as simple as an on-off switch, to a very elaborate automatic electronic thermostat with zone control. Even a wood stove has a control strategy: the occupant. You add another log on the fire when it is needed, and if it gets too hot, you damper the fire or open doors or windows.

Most heating systems today use automatic thermostats for temperature control. Zoning of a house is possible, so that some areas can be warmer than others. Depending on the system, you may use dampers or zone valves to control when and where heat is provided. It is important to note, however, that the temperature difference between zones will be limited unless there is an insulated physical separation between the zones. Without separations, heat will dissipate throughout the house.

The room air temperature thermostat is the most commonly used control. Humidity, air motion and radiation all affect thermal comfort, but most simple heating thermostats measure only the air temperature. Some hydronic systems are also controlled by outdoor temperature sensors.

Thermostats are temperature-operated switches designed to open or close an electrical circuit in response to a temperature change, thus turning the heating system on or off. A good thermostat is essential to obtain the maximum in comfort, convenience and economy of any heating system, while a poor thermostat or control system will cause excessive temperature swings with even the best heating system.

It is also worth mentioning that turning the thermostat up to 90°F when you return to a cold house will not bring the house to a comfortable temperature any quicker than when it is set to the normal comfort setting.

Turning the thermostat up to 90°F will not make the house comfortable any quicker than when it is set to the normal comfort setting. The thermostat is only an on-off switch. The heating system delivers heat at a steady rate regardless the setting.

5. Basic Components of a Heating System

The heating system delivers heat at a steady rate when heat is called for, regardless the setting. Adjusting the thermostat to any setting above the current temperature only turns the heating appliance on.

Residential heating thermostats traditionally have been categorized as low voltage, electronic, and line voltage. New electronic thermostats are blurring the distinctions between the types. Fundamentally, the thermostats are either mechanical or electronic, available as low voltage and line voltage types.

Low Voltage Thermostats

These are the standard thermostats used for central heating systems and unitary systems where more sensitive control is wanted. They operate on a 24V (AC) power source provided by a transformer fed from the standard 240V electric service in the home.

The standard thermostat today for all but electric baseboard heating is a good quality low voltage thermostat with a heat anticipator. The heat anticipator adjusts the cycling rate ("on" and "off" periods) to help reduce temperature swings, and must be adjusted to match the heating appliance it controls.

Line Voltage Thermostats

Line voltage (mechanical or non-electronic) thermostats are generally older style thermostats used exclusively with in-room electric heaters such as baseboards or drop-in heaters. They are simple, inexpensive off/ on switches that conduct full power to the heater. Most are not as efficient and effective as today's newer low voltage and electronic line voltage thermostats.

The inferior line voltage thermostats have a slower response to temperature changes causing a noticeable room temperature swing. The current passing through the thermostat generates heat. This interferes with the proper operation because the thermostat itself heats up, breaks the circuit, and shuts down the heater prematurely. It causes the temperature set point to drop ("droop") during cold weather. The larger the heater and the longer the "on" period, the greater the droop resulting in poor comfort and higher energy costs when you overcompensate by manually adjusting the setting. Some new "diaphragm" line voltage thermostats are more sensitive.

Line voltage thermostats built into the heater are not recommended for normally occupied rooms requiring comfort heating. They only provide thermal comfort conditions at the unit. For better comfort and control, low voltage or electronic line voltage wall mounted thermostats separate from the heater are recommended.

Electronic Line Voltage Thermostats

Electronic thermostats use solid-state components for temperature sensing and switching. They provide very accurate temperature measurement and provide fully proportional control - never fully off and almost never fully on, but hover in-between as directed by the set temperature.

5. Basic Components of a Heating System

Night Setback Thermostats

The simplest night setback control is manual - you turn down the temperature when you go to bed or leave for work, and turn it up when you return or in the morning. More convenient are the programmable or setback thermostats designed to work with a built-in clock. This allows one to sleep in a cool room and get up in a warm one. Night setback allow the temperature to fluctuate to save energy and operating costs. Programmable thermostats are available in line voltage, low voltage and electronic thermostat models. Some have 24 hour, seven days a week program capacity.

However, it is important to note that in energy efficient homes the impact of temperature setbacks is not as significant as it is in a drafty, poorly insulated house. This is because the well-insulated house has a very small heat loss, so it takes a long time to cool down.

In the B.C. Advanced House, a demonstration house built to high energy efficiency levels (with the objective of reducing heating to less than ¼ of conventional houses), measurements were made when the house was unoccupied and the heating system was shut off for one week in January. The interior temperatures dropped an average of less than 4°F (2°C) in 24 hours. The well-insulated building envelope just kept the heat in and solar gains during the day offset most of the heat loss.

In energy efficient homes the impact of temperature setbacks is not as significant as it is in a drafty, poorly insulated house.

Thermostat Location

Thermostats should be mounted on an inside wall about 5 feet above the floor. They should be kept in the open, out from behind doors and drapes, and air circulation around the thermostat should not be too high.

Never put a thermostat on an outside wall, near windows and doors that open to the outside, near a stove, fireplace or heat register or on a wall with pipes or air ducts inside, or any area where a heat-releasing appliance (TV., radio, lamps, etc.) may be found. Also avoid placing a thermostat on either side of a wall exposed to direct sunshine as the extra warmth will mislead the thermostat.

For central heating systems the thermostat should be placed in the most lived-in area. Avoid interior hallways if possible as they are the last to feel outdoor changes. Remember that the only place in the house where you will really have good temperature control is in the area where the thermostat is placed. The rest of the house essentially is a compromise. Comfort is only assured if the distribution of heat is properly laid out to meet the needs of individual rooms.

Home automation systems are beginning to be introduced. These tie heating system controls with other equipment in the house for central computerized control. With these systems, temperature control, humidity, and various appliances can be controlled from a remote location. However, this is a technology that is still emerging.

6. Choosing a heating system

Comfort and Aesthetics

Choosing the best heating system for your home means considering issues not normally associated with heating systems. At the end of this chapter, a worksheet will help you identify those issues most important to you.

Heating system selection is a compromise of first cost and perceived available comfort.

Heating system selection is always a compromise of factors that fall within four broad categories: first cost, comfort, operating costs, and sometimes aesthetics. The importance attached to each will help determine the "best" system for your own situation.

Choosing a heating system used to be easy in the past. You applied a rule of thumb for sizing, and chose a system from a limited selection (as not many alternatives were available). Back then most houses were built in a similar fashion, using similar, relatively small compact designs, and the heat loss varied little from house to house or room to room.

Today most builders put in the heating system they are most familiar with, or is most commonly used in the area. It becomes more complex if you yourself want to carefully consider all relevant features of your house to get the best comfort conditions for the design. Heating systems today are more varied, more complex and more efficient.

Remember that not only homeowners move, but so do contractors and equipment manufacturers. Equipment models become obsolete within a few years. This turnover of homes, occupants, installers, models and manufacturers means that as in other walks of life, constant change is with us.

The basic heating and air-conditioning system should be simple and easily serviced. Complicated systems are more costly to install and service. Equipment should be repairable even by new trades people. However, in the end if you genuinely want better comfort, health, safety, durability and energy efficiency, the search for the best system for your specific application is worth it.

Comfort Issues

Understanding the conditions that are comfortable for you and your family will help narrow down the type of heating system best suited for you. As discussed in chapter 3, comfort conditions vary over the day and year and with occupant age and lifestyles. We may wear different clothes in different seasons. The new born and very old may be less tolerant of wide temperature conditions than a young active family. People with circulatory problems are more susceptible to cold feet or drafts than others.

A good heating system installation can create comfort even in a drafty house. Unfortunately, many systems are not installed to high standards.

Remember that achieving comfort is a shared responsibility of the builder and heating contractor. A very good heating system installation, even in a drafty, multi-level house can create comfort conditions. Unfortunately, most systems are not installed to such high standards.

Lifestyle

Lifestyles and clothing habits are important considerations. If you are used to casual lounging in light clothes and bare feet, a radiant floor heating system may be considered, especially with hard surface floors. If you are usually fully clothed, partial to woolens and always wear footwear, a forced warm air heating system may be suitable.

6. Choosing a heating system

Hands, back of the neck and feet are parts of the body most susceptible to cold. If your feet are cold, you will feel uncomfortable. That is why people who are on their feet all day on an unheated concrete slab, such as sales clerks in shops, can encounter health problems. Similarly, if you or your children often sit or play on the floor your demands may differ from someone who never does. That is where radiant floor heating shines.

House design

The house design, its insulation levels, degree of airtightness, type and size of glass areas and floor materials will affect comfort conditions. Homes that are less airtight, with large glass areas in high vaulted spaces will require special attention to ensure good heat supply and even temperature distribution to these spaces.

House design, insulation levels, airtightness, type and size of windows and floor materials affect comfort conditions.

Big temperature differences between surfaces in a room will have a detrimental impact on comfort and health, especially if surfaces are cold enough to allow condensation to take place. That is why we want well-insulated construction elements.

Large glass areas affect heating system design as the surface temperature of windows is always cooler than other surfaces in the room. As a result, the overall mean radiant temperature is reduced and achieving comfort is more difficult. Heating systems that operate at low temperatures, such as radiant floor or ceiling heating, may not always be able to deliver enough heat to compensate for the high heat losses of the glass areas unless high performance windows are used, or additional heat is provided along these exterior walls.

Building envelopes with low insulation levels will have more heat loss from the house and a lower mean radiant temperature inside. A one level slab-on-grade bungalow has different types of spaces than a large three storey house with 2 or 3-storey high vaulted spaces with a full height window wall. A low-temperature radiant floor or ceiling heating system may be an appropriate or desired system for the slab-on-grade bungalow.

Hard surfaces, especially ceramic tile floors, feel cool to the bare foot. Radiant floor heating of those surfaces, especially in tiled bathrooms, will improve comfort.

A post and beam, open plan home is attractive, but may make it difficult to fit the ducts needed for a forced warm air system. In this type of home incorporating a radiant or baseboard type of system may be easier.

Increasingly we are seeing the use of hybrid systems that incorporate several heat distribution approaches. Thus, we may use a radiant floor or ceiling heat in bathrooms which are ideally kept warm continuously all winter and other tiled areas. Other parts of the house can be heated with forced warm air, which can be set back at night, warm up quickly during the day, and incorporate summer cooling if needed.

6. Choosing a heating system

Heating equipment requires accessible space for the equipment and service.

Space Requirements

We usually forget that most heating equipment requires accessible space for the equipment and service. Most architects and home designers also forget this, as any heating contractor will tell you! Too often, a small closet is all that is given over to mechanical equipment. Space is especially a challenge in small bungalows without basements if forced warm air heating is being installed because sheet metal ducts needed for heating and ventilation take up much space.

A very open, minimalist post and beam type of design may not have enough structure to allow the placement of ducts where they can be boxed out and hidden. Even compact hydronic systems need space for pipes, plumbing headers and valves. As an architect, I admit that on many jobs I have been embarrassed to realize that I have forgotten this basic fact. What it can lead to are dropped ceilings in places where you do not want them, simply because there is no other place to fit the ducts.

Other systems, such as electric radiant (floor or ceiling) and electric baseboards take up no space.

Noise Control

The noise associated with heating equipment can be disturbing, as some people are more sensitive to unwanted sounds than others. A flautist with perfect pitch playing classical music may be very disturbed by the low hum of a boiler pump. An industrial worker or a young person weaned on high volume hard rock music may have no problems with a rattling furnace fan because of his hearing loss. Most often, the noise is a result of oversized furnace installed with undersized ducts.

Heating system noise depends on the number of moving parts, system design, installation, and quality of components.

The noise from a heating system depends on the number of moving parts, system design, installation, and quality of components. Pumps, fans, blowers and moving air will all create noise. Some systems are inherently noisier than others due to the expansion/contraction of elements, vibrations, and flowing water.

Equipment should be placed in an isolated area, furthest away from those areas you want to be most quiet (usually the bedrooms). Older home designs with two stories plus a basement had the mechanical equipment in the basement, with the bedrooms on the top floor, so there was a buffer space between the equipment and the bedrooms.

Mechanical equipment should always be mounted on acoustic isolation mounts, and not hard connected directly to the structure. No matter the quality of equipment, over time a fan or pump can become unbalanced and the equipment will vibrate through the structure, creating a hum somewhere else in the building.

Health (Indoor Air Quality)

Any properly designed and installed heating system that is operating correctly will not have any adverse health implications. Some systems are inherently preferable for maintaining better indoor air quality and for contributing to conditions that reduce allergens in the house.

6. Choosing a heating system

The local furnace installer is usually not an expert in all matters dealing with indoor air pollution. These may be issues such as the impact of smoke, carbon dioxide (CO_2), carbon monoxide (CO), nitrous oxides (NO_x), formaldehyde, radon, volatile organic compounds (VOC), Legionnaires Disease, etc.

If someone in your family has a respiratory problem aggravated by environmental factors such as dust or pollens, the heating system can be designed to reduce levels of those contaminants. For example, if you choose forced air heating, you should install medium efficiency pleated filters to provide control of particulates. If you select a system other than forced warm air, then a separate ducted ventilation system will be needed.

There is a misconception that forced warm air systems are dirty because they move a lot of air. While it is true that dust can be blown around through the ducts, it can also be easily filtered out. However, for filtration to be effective, you must move air past the filter. With an efficient filtration system, forced air heating can actually be one of the cleanest systems you can buy.

High temperature baseboard heating systems can be dirty as they rely on convection currents to move the heat past the baseboard. Fine dust particles in the air may be charred as they pass the heating fins and are deposited on the wall above the baseboard. The hotter the baseboard operating temperature, the more hours it is on, the more noticeable the dust streaking. This is especially visible on light coloured walls as black streaks above the baseboard, and is most pronounced with electric baseboards due to their high temperatures (200°F). Water in hydronic systems often is cooler (typically less than 160°F) so the dust ghosting is less pronounced.

For a person with dust and particle sensitivity, high temperature systems such as electric baseboards could be a problem as the charred dust particles are irritant pollutants. Forced warm air systems also have high temperatures at the furnace, but the air can be filtered.

Systems with combustion chambers open to the house (such as conventional gas furnaces, boilers and water heaters or gas fireplace logs) are subject to occasional spillage of combustion gasses back into the house. Combustion gas spillage can also happen in poorly designed and installed forced warm air heating. If they have leaky ducts, the pressure imbalances that result can draw in combustion products through the return air ducts. Similarly, large exhaust fans (such as large kitchen range hoods or downdraft cooktops) can depressurize the house enough to cause back drafting. For most people a minor isolated incident will not be too serious, but for people who are chemically sensitive, any such incident may be grave. A spillage test can be easily done to ensure safe operation.

Aesthetics

House design and interior decor may play a role in the choice of heating system as some may be more visible to the occupant.

The location and appearance of the heating outlets can be important for some home designs. Forced warm air systems require registers, usually placed in the floor, but they can also be placed on the wall or

There is a misconception that forced warm air systems are dirty ... while it is true that dust can be blown around, it can also be easily filtered out. Remember that the same amounts of dust are generated regardless the heating system. It is not the heating system that generates dust, but people, pets, and their activities.

6. Choosing a heating system

Choosing a Fuel

What is the primary fuel used for space heating in Canada? The main source of energy for forced warm air heating systems is:

natural gas	*70%*
oil	*16%*
electricity	*8%*

In non-forced warm air systems (mostly hydronic heating), it is:

natural gas	*63%*
oil	*22%*
electricity	*13%*

ceiling, especially in better insulated homes. Baseboards and radiators have highly visible three-dimensional elements that may create problems with furniture layout. Radiant systems are invisible.

Choosing a Fuel

Choice of fuel depends on local availability, cost, convenience, supply security, environmental impact, safety, cleanliness, annual maintenance requirements, equipment preference, system efficiency and availability of service technicians. Consider alternative fuels that might be used in the future. In the recent past we have seen upheavals that have changed energy availability and pricing. Many houses more than 30 years old today have switched the primary heating fuel type from that used when first built. How long will the fuel supply last? Consider future pollution reduction legislation that may affect the fuel source.

My own home, where I am sitting and writing this book, has over its life seen four fuel types. When first built in 1911, it was heated with wood or sawdust. Some time later an oil furnace was installed, and replaced by a gas heated furnace in the early 1960's. In the last renovations just a few years ago I used a new, high efficiency gas heater in combination with solar energy (both active and passive).

Electric and gas utilities have a basic service charge that is applied to your bill whether or not you use any energy. The actual energy use is charged on top. Also, keep in mind that some utilities have variable pricing structures. Prices may vary with time of day, time of year or quantity of energy purchased. You also have varying appliance efficiencies. Thus the cost of the heat provided in the room must take into account the cost of the fuel (with service charges) along with the system efficiency.

Recent market deregulation in many areas means there may a confusing array of pricing structures to tempt prospective customers. This may complicate fuel price comparison and fuel choice decisions if made on price considerations only.

Electricity

In areas with abundant sources of secure low cost hydro generated electricity it offers a viable heating-energy option for homes. In areas reliant on coal, nuclear or oil fired thermal generation for electricity, the environmental costs are high, so electrical use should be reduced to the minimum and not used for space heating unless absolutely necessary.

Electricity is sold by the kilowatt hour.

6. Choosing a heating system

Electricity

Advantages

☞ Usually a low initial cost, easy installation

☞ Takes up little space as no vents, combustion air or fuel storage are required

☞ Wide range of equipment, from a central furnace or boiler to individual room heaters

☞ Electric service easily located

☞ Single utility service charge

☞ Low maintenance costs as systems have few moving parts

Disadvantages

☞ High operating costs in areas where low cost natural gas, oil or wood is available

☞ Subject to interruption in power outages

☞ Larger panel and service required

☞ Environmentally costly if electricity is generated by thermal plants using coal, diesel, natural gas or nuclear fuels

☞ Places peak load demands on many utilities

Natural gas

Natural gas, where it is available, is usually the most economical fuel source. Energy efficient appliances should always be considered to reduce the amount consumed, because unlike electricity, where its heating efficiency is 100%, the efficiency of natural gas or any other fossil fuel is always less than 100%.

Natural gas burns more cleanly than any of the other fossil fuels. Combustion gases are mostly CO_2, water vapour, small quantities of nitrous oxides (NO_x) and waste heat which can not be recovered. However, CO_2 and NO_x are greenhouse gases that contribute to global warming. There are also significant external inefficiencies in the total gas delivery system, when gas well exploration, wellhead burn off, and pipeline efficiencies are considered.

It is metered by volume, then converted to the unit by which it is priced. In B.C. natural gas is sold by energy units (gigajoules). Other utilities sell it by volume (cubic feet, cubic meters) (etc.). Older meters measure in cubic feet; new meters measure in cubic meters.

The energy content of natural gas can vary, but is usually about 1000 BTU per cubic foot.

Therms and decatherms are imperial (US) measures of energy.

Natural Gas

Advantages

☞ Generally is the least costly fuel source, per unit of energy

☞ Wide variety of equipment is available

☞ Easy to install and service

☞ Fuel can be used for other household appliances (cooking, dryers)

☞ Very energy efficient appliances available.

☞ Some fireplaces and ranges function even during a power outage.

Disadvantages

☞ Requires combustion air and vents, taking up space and making sealing the house more difficult

☞ Improper installation or damage could, in extreme cases, cause an explosion.

☞ Generally means a second utility service charge for the home

☞ Contributes greenhouse gases as a product of combustion.

☞ When malfunctioning, combustion gases can spill into the house

---

6. Choosing a heating system

Propane

Propane is closely related to natural gas. It is shipped and stored in pressurized tanks and is used where gas features are wanted in areas without access to natural gas. Most natural gas appliances can be used with small modifications to adapt to propane. Sometimes, propane is used in areas where gas pipelines are scheduled to be installed within a few years of construction of the house.

Propane is heavier than air so a leak can pool on the floor, creating a safety hazard.

Propane is a gas when it is burned, but is sold in a liquid form in pressurized containers by volume (usually litres) or by weight. Propane has a higher heat content than natural gas, with an energy content of about 2500 BTU/cu.ft, but usually costs about three times as much per unit of energy.

Propane
Advantages
- High heat content
- Wide variety of equipment is available (natural gas appliances can be used with adjustments)
- Generally easy to install and service
- Fuel can be used for other household appliances (cooking, dryers)
- Very energy efficient appliances available.
- Some fireplaces and stoves function even during a power outage.

Disadvantages
- High operating costs due to high fuel price
- Moderate initial costs and maintenance
- Requires combustion air and vents taking up space, and making sealing the house more difficult
- Improper installation or damage to system could cause an explosion.
- Contributes greenhouse gases as a product of combustion.
- When malfunctioning, combustion gases can spill into the house

Oil

In areas away from gas distribution grids, oil provides a reasonable alterative and in some areas its use is increasing. Although this fossil fuel has its environmental costs, it is easily storable and transportable, eliminating the need for an extensive pipeline grid or special pressure storage tanks.

Oil
Advantages
- Equipment with good operating efficiencies is available
- Generally easy to install and service
- Storage tanks easy to handle
- A storable fuel source does not impose peak demands on utility grid system

Disadvantages
- Fuel storage tank required
- High operating and maintenance costs
- Oil is smelly
- Limited range of appliances available
- Requires combustion air and vents taking up space, and making sealing the house more difficult
- Contributes greenhouse gases as a product of combustion.
- When malfunctioning, combustion gases can spill into the house
- Equipment requires regular maintenance

6. Choosing a heating system

Oil contains complex constituents including volatile oils, so there are persistent odours around the storage tank and heating units that are difficult to remove from the home. Some people are very sensitive to these odours.

The heat content of a litre of No. 2 fuel oil is about 37,000 BTU. A common measure for engineering practice is 140,000 BTU per US gallon.

Wood

Wood has regained some popularity as a heat source in recent years. However, remember that a subsequent owner may not have your enthusiasm for the extra work involved to stoke the wood stove! If wood is being considered, a reliable long term source of fuel wood is required. This may not always be the case everywhere, especially in urban areas.

A major concern about wood as a fuel is its potential to contribute to air pollution. As a result, some areas have introduced regulations restricting the use of wood burning appliances. Smoldering smoky fires produce visible smoke and pollute the air. They are an indication of incomplete combustion and wasted wood. For maximum efficiency, and minimum pollution, the fire must be burned hot, without allowing it to smolder.

Wood burning efficiency depends on its moisture content. Under cover wood dries at the rate of one inch per year. Higher temperatures will dry wood faster. A solar wood drying shed can easily be constructed by enclosing a traditional wood shed in recycled glass or plastic and allowing good air flows. A six-inch diameter log takes three years to dry completely. Wood should never be stored or dried inside the house.

Wood should never be stored or dried inside the house.

The heat content of wood varies depending on species and moisture content. Hardwood typically has a heat content of about 29,000,000 BTU/cord (30,600 MJ/cord), while for softwood it is about 17,000,000 BTU/cord (18,700 MJ/cord).

Wood

Advantages
- ☞ Low operating costs
- ☞ Low cost fuel source in some areas
- ☞ Does not rely on electrical power
- ☞ Wide variety of equipment is available
- ☞ Low environmental impact if sustainably managed wood is available

Disadvantages
- ☞ More dangerous than some other fuels if appliances are not maintained properly
- ☞ Higher initial cost especially if combined with other fuels
- ☞ Fuel storage and preparation required
- ☞ Requires a chimney for venting and a combustion air supply
- ☞ Precise temperature control is not always possible
- ☞ Can affect air quality both indoors and outdoors
- ☞ High maintenance
- ☞ Creates environmental pollution if not properly maintained or burned
- ☞ Contributes greenhouse gases as a product of combustion
- ☞ When malfunctioning, combustion gases can spill into the house
- ☞ Increased insurance rates

---

6. Choosing a heating system

Solar Energy

The sun is an inexhaustible energy source. It is the source of all life on earth. As a heating fuel for buildings it has not been considered seriously until recently. It can be used in all areas year round, for both space and water heating. Solar use requires careful design and should not be considered a direct substitution for conventional energy sources (oil, propane or grid supplied). Its use has to recognize daily and annual movements of the sun.

The further north one goes, the bigger an issue this becomes as the position of the sun and its intensity will change significantly over the year. For example, at 54°N latitude (e.g., Edmonton), the noonday sun will be 58° above the horizon in July but only 14° in December. At 45°N (e.g., Ottawa), it will be 66° above the horizon in July, and 24° in December.

Solar Energy

Advantages
- ☞ Energy supply is infinite
- ☞ Low energy costs
- ☞ Passive systems generally do not entail extra costs
- ☞ Clean fuel
- ☞ Environmentally the most appropriate energy source
- ☞ Passive systems not reliant on electrical power supply
- ☞ Good for the spirit when winter sun can penetrate house

Disadvantages
- ☞ May require design modifications prior to construction
- ☞ Highly variable availability
- ☞ At northern latitudes will not provide all space heating needs
- ☞ Active solar systems can be expensive and may not provide all energy needs
- ☞ Requires thermal storage

Fuel Comparison

How does one compare these various fuels? The following table provides a price comparison for an equivalent amount of heat supplied by the various fuels. Each has been converted to 1 Gigajoule of useful heat (approximately 1,000,000 BTU) at the most common rates of conversion efficiency. Prices are based on approximate BC energy costs at time of publication. Where prices are significantly different, you can adjust the cost by the ratio of price difference. (e.g. if the cost of electricity is $0.12/kWhr, or twice the cost, then the cost per gigajoule will be twice that in the table, or $33.36).

Energy Cost Comparisons			
Fuel	Efficiency	Fuel cost	$ per GJ
Natural Gas	80%	$5.40/GJ	$6.75
	90%	$5.40/GJ	$6.00
	80%	$9.09/GJ	$11.36
Electricity	100%	$0.06/kWh	$16.68
Propane	80%	$0.42/litre	$19.74
	90%	$0.42/litre	$17.54
Oil	70%	$0.35/litre	$12.90
	80%	$0.35/litre	$11.28
Wood	50%	$100/chord	$11.80

6. Choosing a heating system

Efficiency of Operation

Everyone wants a low operating cost heating system. Fuel burning appliances always lose some of their heat through the chimney or by inefficiencies of combustion. The amount of useable heat determines the appliance's efficiency. It can vary anywhere from 0% or less (i.e., a net loss) for older conventional fireplaces, to 50-60% for conventional gas furnaces or boilers up to 95% for modern high efficiency units.

When comparing fuel costs, you must consider the fuel cost per BTU, overall system efficiency and also fuel supplier service charges. Just because your furnace is rated at 80%, and the fuel cost is $1.00 per unit, does not mean that the cost of the energy will be $1.25. There are system inefficiencies, plus the utility service charges. However, in the case of electricity, the service charge is not considered for heating cost calculations because the assumption is that electricity is provided first for lights and appliances.

Most building codes do not regulate overall heating system efficiency standards. However, equipment-specific efficiency standards are set and regulated by federal and provincial bodies. There are two types of efficiency ratings on fuel fired appliances: steady state efficiency and annual fuel utilization efficiency (AFUE).

Building codes do not regulate overall heating system efficiency standards.

Electric heaters (baseboard or furnace) are considered 100% efficient because they convert all the electricity they draw to heat. Electric boilers and furnaces lose 10 - 15% distribution efficiency depending on where they are located. A very efficient furnace or boiler put into a poorly designed distribution system may not deliver good system efficiency.

Coefficient of Performance (COP) measures electric heating equipment efficiency. A COP of 1 means the heat energy that the appliance delivers is the same as the electrical energy it consumes. Heat pump equipment usually has a COP greater than 1 - up to about 4 for ground source (geothermal) units with a big in-ground heat exchanger loop.

Combustion or steady state efficiency is determined by comparing the heat output with the fuel input. Input is the amount of fuel burned or consumed by an appliance. For example if a furnace has an input rating of 100,000 BTU/hr then the furnace will burn fuel at the rate of 100,000 BTU per hour. Output is the amount of useable heat energy available, and is used to calculate appliance efficiency. If the name plate says input 100,000 BTU, and output is 75,000 you have a 75% combustion efficiency appliance. Ninety-five percent is about the highest combustion efficiency that is achievable for natural gas, propane or oil.

This efficiency rating measures only what happens during the combustion process when the fire is at its optimum. Other factors that must be considered include standby losses due to continuous pilot lights, radiated losses, warm-up periods, and warm house air that goes up the chimney between heating cycles. These are considered into a calculation for seasonal efficiency, which is always lower than combustion efficiency. For example, gas water heaters usually have a combustion efficiency of about 70%, which is what you may see on promotional literature, but the

6. Choosing a heating system

seasonal efficiency is about 54% for a 30 gallon tank. That is a substantial difference. Older water heaters may typically be 45 - 50%, except for a few specially designed systems.

Gas furnaces with an efficiency rating of 83% or more are called condensing units because to extract the maximum amount of heat, a secondary heat exchanger extracts heat from the flue gases. The water vapour in the exhaust is condensed thus releasing additional heat. The condensate is mildly acidic and corrosive. All furnace parts contacting the condensate must be able to withstand the acidity.The exhaust flue is typically a plastic pipe (PVC) rated for higer temperature use. Early models had problems relating to corrosion, but these have now been resolved.

Higher efficiency units have advantages beyond burning fuel more efficiently. All units have a fan to exhaust combustion gases. In some units the combustion is sealed in a chamber, drawing combustion air directly from outdoors, and also exhausting combustion products outside. Because these units are sealed and fan powered, they provide greater separation of house air from combustion products, increasing safety.

An annual fuel utilization rating (AFUE) was developed to simulate realistic seasonal operating conditions. The AFUE is a rating like the performance ratings for automobiles. It is based on test conditions, but tries to simulate average use conditions that include on-and-off cycling. Every time the appliance fires up but before it reaches full operating conditions and again when it shuts off and starts to cool down, there will be a loss of operating efficiency. The AFUE of a mid-efficiency gas furnace is about 80% while a high efficiency gas furnace is about 92 - 95% efficient.

Annual fuel utilization rating (AFUE) is a rating like the miles per gallon ratings for automobiles... it is based on test conditions, but tries to simulate average use conditions.

Furnace motor power consumption is not part of the equipment efficiency calculations. This is a concern, because furnaces today are often run continuously to provide ventilation air distribution and air circulation within the house. Until recently, most of the furnace fan motors have been very inefficient, consuming much power. An inefficient motor can easily consume 1800 kWh or more of electricity per year. At some times of the year, the heat given off by the blower motor can overheat a very energy efficient house (adding to the cooling load if cooling is needed).

The most commonly used furnace fan motor type today is a permanent split capacitor (PSC). The most efficient motors are electronically commutated motors (ECM). Other names used for similar more efficient motors are integrated control motor (ICM) and electronic frequency modulation (EFM). The argument in favour of the ECM motors becomes stronger where summer cooling is a consideration. Because these motors run much cooler, they do not rob the efficiency of the cooling system.

Generally, the more efficient the equipment, the higher the capital cost. Furnaces with the high efficiency motors can add a premium of up to $1,000. Are they worth it? The added cost must be considered along with better performance, quieter blowers and lower operating costs.

Minimum efficiency	
Gas furnaces	78 % (AFUE)
Gas water heater	.57 (EF)
Oil water heater	.54 (EF)
Ground source heat pump:	
All units	COP 3 (Closed loop units COP 2.5)

Gas and oil water heaters typically have a steady state efficiency in the 70-75% range, but that is only the conversion efficiency. System losses from other components mean the net efficiency is much lower - usually in the 45-50% range.

6. Choosing a heating system

If the furnace is run simply on a demand cycle (i.e., turned on only when heat is called for) the number of hours the furnace will run may be 1,500-2,000 hours per year, so the savings are modest - maybe $40-50 per year at an electric rate of $0.06/kWh. However, if the furnace fan is run continuously, as it will be if it is used to distribute ventilation air and filter the air, the savings increase to $150 or more per year. The incremental cost for the better furnace becomes much more attractive.

Remember that with electricity there are external system inefficiencies for generating and delivering the electricity. If the electricity is generated by coal or gas fired plants (as in Alberta, Ontario, Nova Scotia and Saskatchewan) there is a significant loss of efficiency in the overall system, although that is never factored into any system calculations. If you consider the losses in generation and transmission, about ⅔ of the energy content of the fuel is lost. In other words, thermal electricity is only 33% efficient at converting the energy. (That is one reason electricity is usually the most expensive fuel).

Hydro generated electricity is much more efficient, but never 100%, as there are transmission losses in getting the electricity from the generating facility to the house.

Maintenance

No matter the quality of the equipment, all systems require maintenance. Generally the more parts there are, the more maintenance will be required. Filters have to be cleaned or changed, pumps and motors serviced, combustion chambers checked, flues cleaned where oil or wood is used and controls safety checked.

Maintenance instructions should be in simple language, mounted on the wall near the equipment, and protected so that they will last 15 or 20 years.

No matter the quality of the equipment, all systems require maintenance.

Ease of Installation

Installation is a concern for the owner, heating contractor and builder. Some heating systems are more directly tied to the design and construction of the house than others. For example, most radiant and passive solar systems are built right into the structure of the house, while electric baseboard heaters can be added later. Large open areas and heavy timber frames and exposed beams make installing heating and ventilation ducts a real challenge.

Combustion Gas Venting and Combustion Air Requirements

Heating appliances that burn fuels must be provided with combustion air and combustion products must be vented out of the house. Older equipment found in most houses today is naturally (gravity) vented. This means the combustion air is taken from surrounding areas open to the house and

6. Choosing a heating system

natural buoyancy of hot air is relied on to generate the draft up and out the chimney to remove combustion products. Most mid efficiency appliances are not direct vented, but must be installed with separate combustion air supply.

Fireplaces and wood stoves similarly require combustion air. Where and how the combustion air is brought into the house has to be considered along with how combustion gases are to be exhausted. These appliances draw their combustion air from their immediate area and depend on its replacement by active or passive air inlets from the exterior.

Newer high efficiency units are power or direct vented. They have a duct that provides combustion air directly into the fire box and exhaust gases are directly vented to the outside, usually with a powered fan that draws the gases out. These sealed combustion appliances are highly recommended for use in new well-insulated energy efficient homes.

Safety (back drafting)

Naturally vented combustion appliances (with open flames) can spill combustion gasses back into the house if excessive negative pressures are generated in the house, as may happen when large exhaust fans are turned on. In extreme cases this can be fatal to the residents.

It goes without saying that all systems must be safe. There are features that make some heating systems more vulnerable to malfunctions than others. Naturally vented combustion appliances, with open flames, are subject to problems when excessive negative pressures are generated in the house and combustion gases are spilled back into the house (back drafted). A variety of toxic gases, including carbon monoxide (CO) can be drawn into the living space. If this malfunction is combined with chimney spillage or complete reversal the heating system can be lethal.

As CO is a toxic, colourless gas, there is no way a person can detect unsafe CO levels. Ontario requires that carbon monoxide detectors be installed where a wood burning appliance is installed. However, wood burning appliances are not the only ones capable of producing CO.

I am familiar with one case where a new sealed combustion furnace failed within three years of installation. It had spewed deadly carbon monoxide gas into the house for many weeks, but because it is a colourless, odourless gas, the malfunction was only discovered when the furnace stopped working. By that time the levels in the house had been at toxic levels (164 ppm) for some time (background levels are 2-3 ppm, and anything above 11 ppm over several hours is a cause for concern).

I always recommend that a CO detector be used any time that combustion appliances are present in a home.

I now always recommend that a CO detector be used any time that combustion appliances are used in a home. The detector would normally be installed in the main living area of the house.

Who Designs the Heating System?

Heating systems in houses have generally been sized and designed by "rule of thumb" by the installing contractor, unlike the situation in large buildings, where mechanical engineers always design heating and cooling systems and take responsibility for them. Some mechanical engineers do design work for small houses, as do some architects and technologists who specialize in residential work.

6. Choosing a heating system

Unfortunately, training in heating system design is not a normal part of the training programs of the trades that install heating systems. These include electricians, plumbers, gas fitters, and sheet metal trades. Some may have taken special courses or workshops and can design residential heating systems. Younger trades persons with a technology diploma may have received some formal training.

Training in heating system design is not a normal part of the training programs of the trades that install heating systems.

However, in our cost conscious society, contracts are usually awarded to the lowest bidder. Because inspection of heating system installation is almost non-existent, and heating equipment manufacturers are mainly driven by numbers, the quality of installed systems follow suit.

Many equipment wholesalers and some heating contractors offer heat loss and design services to their customers. However, the contractors only do the design after they are awarded the contract.

Quality contractors or technicians can design a system and do a very good layout. They can also offer insights based on practical experience. Sometimes, their practical experience is extremely valuable on its own. However, if they only deal with one type of heating system, you may not get the benefit of an impartial evaluation or commentary about other heating options.

Building heat loss and heating system design should be done before construction. If the person doing the heat loss calculations does not have detailed construction specifications, they will make assumptions about the building envelope components. For example, if your house has large window areas and you have opted to use the best high performance windows (such as Heat Mirror™ with an overall R value of 4.6) and extra insulation on the walls, but the heating designer based the system on standard glass, and minimum code insulation levels, there could be a significant mismatch between the calculated heat load and what is actually required.

Ask your heating contractor who will be doing the heat loss analysis and designing the heating system?

Regardless whether or not the design service is offered for "free" you will be paying for this service. If it is "free" the cost is simply added into the cost of the hardware and installation. If you have any concerns or uncertainty about the heating system, do consult with an independent consultant that will not have a stake in the choice of finished product.

If you are not dealing with a design professional who can offer heating system design, the local home builders' association, heating trade associations, or utility can offer references. Even a mechanical engineer who does not handle residential work may be willing to consult on an hourly basis, to review the concepts or design supplied by a contractor. However, you should be aware that some utilities now maintain lists of preferred contractors who pay a commission for referrals, so their recommendation may only be to a contractor willing to pay the fee.

How Much Will it Cost?

When we mention heating systems, the second question usually is how much and what is the "payback" of an efficient heating system. However, we never seem to question the payback of a kitchen cabinet, a

6. Choosing a heating system

Unlike other systems in the house, the heating system has an ongoing operating cost. Over the life time of the heating system the operating costs are by far the most significant, even when you consider financing costs.

All the important comfort, health and safety issues we are discussing in this book do not readily translate into cost figures.

plumbing fixture, or doorknobs. While we can put a price to the hardware and installation, the cost-benefit of thermal comfort cannot be quantified easily.

As a proportion of the total cost of construction, today's heating systems are a bargain. The costs for heating systems typically represent less than 5% of construction costs. Twenty or thirty years ago, a simple heating system often cost about 10% of the total cost of a house.

Usually, the more you spend initially, the less you will pay on an ongoing basis. All the important comfort, health and safety issues we are discussing in this book do not readily translate into cost figures.

The biggest portion of the cost of a heating system, and the hardest for the unfamiliar person to evaluate is the installation labour. When you are making a selection, it is tempting to look only at the initial capital cost. After all, that is the immediate impact your bank account will see. Unlike other systems and products in the house, the heating system has an ongoing operating cost for maintenance and energy used. There are two aspects to costs - the initial capital cost of the system, normally amortized over the 20-year life of the system, and the ongoing operating costs. Over the life time of the heating system the operating costs are by far the most significant. The only possible exception is the geothermal heat pump.

Capital Costs

When analysing the heating system costs, consider also the impact of other construction costs. In other words, what are the consequences of upgrading insulation levels and using higher performance windows on the heating system cost?

When reviewing capital costs, don't forget to include the cost of floor space used by the heating system that could be used for other purposes. As well, other necessary elements of a system need to be considered, such as framing around ducts, flues, chimneys, wood shed, oil tank and hook-up fees to the gas or hydro system. With a super insulated passive solar heated house designed to collect all the heat needed, will an automatic back-up system still be required by the building inspector or the bank?

Some systems have other indirect costs that are directly associated with the system that may not always be quoted in the price. One example: the mechanical contractor sells the materials and labour to install the pumps, pipes, controls, etc. for a floor radiant system and provides a price for that work, but the thermal mass that should be placed over a wood subfloor is handled by a separate trade, as is gas fitting and controls installation, so it may not appear in the quotation.

If you are quoted an exceptionally low price, you may be tempted to consider it your lucky day. However, if you are paying much less than the local yardsticks suggest is the cost for that type of system, you are very likely not getting the quality of materials and installation necessary. Wrong decisions made can be costly, because unlike the replacement of a

6. Choosing a heating system

faulty floor covering or lighting fixture, repairs to heating systems may have major structural consequences. It is not easy to bring a substandard system initially installed up to a good quality.

Any quote that varies by more than 20% from the mean should be considered as suspect.

If the price looks too good to be true, it probably is!

Operating Costs

We understand capital costs - the cost of purchasing and installing the equipment. Operating costs can be far more important, especially if you plan to stay in the house for a while. The operating costs are not seen until after you move in and start to get the bills - and they will continue as long as you live in the house. Paying a bit extra up front for higher quality equipment and, what is more important, good installation can yield longer term savings.

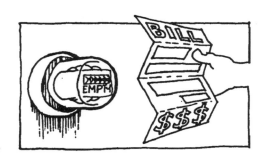

The total annual operating cost should include amortization of capital, fuel cost, chimney cleaning, maintenance, and additional insurance (if applicable). Some systems (e.g., wood or pellet burning systems) have other costs that may include: wood cutting and hauling, chainsaw, truck, upkeep, etc. Is the time needed to run the system worth anything to you?

It is worth recognizing that there are measurable pay-backs to be had with efficient systems and energy efficient home construction that reduces the amount of energy needed. That is one reason that some financial institutions will give you a break on an R-2000 house. Even if you do not have a certified R-2000 house, but if you can show that the operating costs will be lower, you should be able to negotiate a better deal on the financing.

To find out what the pay-back will be by selecting a more efficient appliance, based on fuel costs, you need to estimate the annual heating energy consumption for your house, the energy costs and the efficiencies of the heating appliances you are considering.

Most energy utilities have sample calculations for operating costs for a typical house in their service area. They are an approximation based on local energy prices.

We have presented a sample calculation based on a typical condition in Vancouver and Kamloops.

Annual Fuel Cost Comparison				
Assumed fuel price	Electricity $0.06/kwhr	Natural Gas* $ 5.40/GJ	Propane $ 0.42/litre	Oil $ 0.35/litre
Insulation Levels				
Vancouver, BC				
Standard building code construction	$ 1144	$ 577	$ 1094	$ 972
National Energy Code standard	$ 955	$ 544	$ 914	$ 814
R-2000 standard	$ 452	$ 244	$ 443	$ 379
Kamloops, BC				
Standard building code construction	$ 1380	$ 670	$ 1321	$ 1184
National Energy Code standard	$ 1262	$ 610	$ 1208	$ 993
R-2000 standard	$ 629	$ 305	$ 640	$ 522

* assumes 80% efficient furnace

Energy prices usually have added surcharges for tank rentals, basic billing charges, taxes, etc.

The prices in the table reflect 1999 energy prices in BC. They provide a relative relationship between fuels. For other prices, adjustment can be made by prorating to local prices.

6. Choosing a heating system

It becomes more difficult to compare different distribution systems. For example, a mid-efficiency forced warm air furnace compared with a high-efficiency boiler for a hydronic radiant floor system are two distinct system types. You can compare the quantity of energy each consumes, but the capital costs of the systems will vary. More importantly, the *qualities* of each are different.

Warranty

Warranties are usually equipment manufacturer warranties only. These typically cover only the equipment; if the furnace or boiler fails, the manufacturer replaces or repairs it at their discretion, based on the warranty details. However, the warranty usually does not cover the cost of the freight, labour and (if applicable) permits. Most installers offer a one year labour warranty at no cost.

Consider the credibility and resources of the equipment manufacturer. Is the equipment new technology being developed by a small entrepreneurial company, or is it made by a large national or multinational company that has been in business for many years? Much of the more interesting innovative development work is done by small, sometimes undercapitalized companies. Their products should not be dismissed as a result. It could well be superior in quality and performance to more established "name brand" products, but there is a risk associated with it in the event a problem emerges a few years after installation. They may not have the resources, if they are still in business, to correct the problem, in which case new replacement equipment would have to be purchased at full market price.

Heating Contractor Credibility

Installer experience, credibility and warranties must be considered. What kind of warranty does the heating contractor offer? Indeed, will the contractor still be around? Many contractors these days work out of a truck with a phone - seemingly without any permanent address. These contractors may well be cheaper, but that lower price may come without a meaningful warranty service. A storefront doesn't automatically guarantee quality and good service either.

Always check contractor references and credentials.

Check contractor references and credentials. How long has he been in business? Have they done projects like yours before? Do they do their own service work or contract it out? Have they asked you a lot of questions about the house and your lifestyle, so they can determine your needs?

Ask what kind of training their people have. Do they take ongoing training courses and seminars when they are available? If they do, they will proudly tell you about this. If they don't, or try to tell you why the courses are not worth it, it should tell you that they may be uncomfortable with the line of questioning.

6. Choosing a heating system

Are they members of trade associations? Trade association membership is no guarantee of quality and standards, but it does tell you that they are sufficiently interested in their industry's professionalism to participate in industry activities.

Consider buying from the person that asks you the most questions.

Impact on Resale Value

Whether or not you are building for resale, you may want to keep in mind the perception about heating systems in your area. As we know, buying decisions are not always based on rational analysis, but may often be made purely on gut feelings, emotions, nostalgia, social focus, aesthetics, or prejudices. Accordingly, a heating system that is not common in the area may not mean much to a subsequent purchaser, and could in fact be a liability.

For example, if you opt for a wood heater, especially in the middle of an urban area, the potential number of buyers willing to deal with firewood may be limited.

In some heating-only climates, radiant heating has become so popular, that builders feel obliged to use radiant whether or not it really is the best system for a given home. It is just that many people have been sold on radiant as the heating system of choice, supposedly because it is cleaner and more efficient than forced warm air (although as we will show, that may not necessarily be the case). The next part of the book gets into more detail about specific system types.

6. Choosing a heating system

Evaluation Criteria Worksheet

Selecting your heating system may not be easy and will entail compromises. No simple formula can be designed for you to plug in a few numbers, to come up with a simple decision. There is never one perfect, "best" heating system.

The following worksheet gives you an opportunity to identify heating system features important to you. Then, when you review heating system types, you can decide which of those will best meet your specific preferences.

1. What system features are important to you, and how important is this feature to you?

	High	medium	low
Comfort and aesthetic considerations	☐	☐	☐
Warm floors	☐	☐	☐
Uniform temperatures in the house	☐	☐	☐
Minimized drafts	☐	☐	☐
Noise control	☐	☐	☐
Ability to deal with allergy problems	☐	☐	☐
Total flexibility of furniture placement	☐	☐	☐
Clean system operation	☐	☐	☐
Air filtration	☐	☐	☐
Allergy design considerations	☐	☐	☐
Humidity control	☐	☐	☐
Air conditioning (cooling)	☐	☐	☐
Appearance of fittings	☐	☐	☐

2. Fuel Choice. Identify the most important options for you. (Not all fuels may be available or appropriate for your situation).

	Electric	Natural Gas	Propane	Oil	Wood	Solar	Other
Local availability	☐	☐	☐	☐	☐	☐	☐
Cost of fuel	☐	☐	☐	☐	☐	☐	☐
Convenience	☐	☐	☐	☐	☐	☐	☐
Supply security	☐	☐	☐	☐	☐	☐	☐
Environmental impact	☐	☐	☐	☐	☐	☐	☐
Equipment preference and lifespan	☐	☐	☐	☐	☐	☐	☐
Equipment and system efficiency	☐	☐	☐	☐	☐	☐	☐
Annual maintenance requirements	☐	☐	☐	☐	☐	☐	☐
Safety	☐	☐	☐	☐	☐	☐	☐
Cleanliness	☐	☐	☐	☐	☐	☐	☐

Are there several fuel options available? _____

Preferred fuel choice _____

6. Choosing a heating system

Technical considerations	Yes	No
Are there large glass areas in the house?	☐	☐
Are the floors mainly:		
soft surfaces (carpets)?	☐	☐
hard surfaces (tile, wood, concrete)?	☐	☐
Is there a reasonable space for mechanical equipment?	☐	☐
Is the design an open plan?	☐	☐
Is the house divided into many different rooms?	☐	☐
Are there places to conceal ducts?	☐	☐
Is temperature zoning important (individual room or zone control)?	☐	☐
Does it matter if there are visible elements (registers, baseboards, panels)	☐	☐
Is there an open fireplace?	☐	☐
Is ease of servicing important?	☐	☐
Is ease of installation important?	☐	☐
Are there qualified personnel available for installation and service?	☐	☐
Is space limited for mechanical equipment?	☐	☐
Does it have to integrate with ventilation?	☐	☐
Would a combination of systems work best?	☐	☐

Financial	High	Moderate	Low
How important are the following elements:			
Is the total system cost important?	☐	☐	☐
Maintenance and service costs?	☐	☐	☐
Operating costs?	☐	☐	☐
Installer warranties?	☐	☐	☐

	Yes	No
Are there other costs associated with the system?	☐	☐
Must it add to resale value to the home?	☐	☐
Is a warranty from the manufacturer important?	☐	☐
Are previous customer references important?	☐	☐

7. Heating system types

Each heating system has its unique characteristics. We describe various heating system options available, and offer comments on each.

The most common heating system types in Canadian homes today are:

forced warm air systems	*45.8%*
electric baseboards	*26.7%*
central hot water systems	*13.9%*
wood stoves	*7.4%*
heat pumps	*2.9%*
others	*3.3%*

(radiant heating is identified in 1.4% of houses).

It is worth remembering that as recently as seventy years ago only the wealthy could enjoy the comfort and quality of indoor environment that today is considered commonplace.

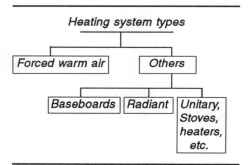

Many different types of heating systems can provide a comfortable, healthy home environment in an efficient manner.

Often there is confusion between heating system type, fuel source and heat distribution methods. Many different heating products are available on the market, just as there are a variety of fuel types. "Electric heating" or "natural gas" do not of themselves define a heating system type. They define the energy source.

There are two basic categories of heating systems: forced warm air and others that are non-forced warm air. We have broken down the discussion of heating systems in this fashion because, as will become clearer in chapter 9, it defines how a ventilation system is selected.

Forced warm air systems deliver heat through a network of ducts throughout the house. A fan is used to move the air through these ducts.

Non-forced warm air systems deliver heat through pipes, radiators, or cables but without the fans and ducts of a forced air system. They may have a central heater or boiler, as in hydronic systems, or be a single heater such as an electric baseboard, radiant panel or wood stove.

Forced warm air is often improperly considered dusty, drafty, noisy, inefficient and smelly, while non-forced warm air systems are often considered cleaner, dust free, more efficient, quieter. These are common misconceptions. In the following sections we will show why they are not correct. The concern people usually have for a given system type is based on experience with poorly installed or maintained heating systems. Only when something has gone wrong do we become aware of a problem. If it contributes to discomfort, we tend to blame the heating system itself.

Remember that each heating system has its unique qualities, and has to be designed and installed correctly. A good understanding of the characteristics of each will help to dispel myths and give you a basis on which you can select the type of heating you may want to have in your home.

Forced Warm Air Systems

Forced warm air systems consist of a furnace to heat the air and ductwork to distribute the warmed air through the house. Besides supplying heat, a forced warm air system can also provide ventilation, air circulation, filtration, humidification and air cooling.

Heat Source

Heat is provided by a furnace, fan coil or heat pump. A blower moves air through the heat exchanger where it is heated.

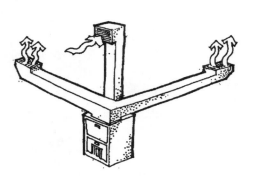

7. Heating system types

Distribution

Heat is distributed by the blower to a system of ducts. The forced convection creates a movement of warm air that blankets the outside walls and windows.

New furnaces are available with two-stage blowers and two-stage burners, so that as more heat is called for, the air flow and flame is increased. Supply and return sheet metal ducts connect the furnace with the various rooms in the house. The amount of air that can be moved through a duct depends on the duct size, the driving force pushing the air, the duct length, and the number of fittings such as elbows, splices, junctions, registers, etc.

Return ducts are typically a combination of sheet metal ducts and wall or floor cavities. An effective system will have matched supply and return air flows from all parts of the house, and all ducts will be made of sheet metal and sealed at all joints. Sometimes construction cavities are used as ducts but they cannot always provide this accurate air flow with certainty and dust and debris can be moved into the house when these cavities are made part of the air circulation system.

Controls

Forced warm air systems generally have treated the whole house as a single zone, controlled by a single thermostat placed in a central location of the house. If you wanted some rooms cooler, the warm air register had to be closed. Zone control capable of providing up to 4 temperature zones is now available for forced air heating systems.

Costs

The average cost of an installed forced warm air heating system is about $1.10 - $1.60 per square foot of house floor area.

Other Considerations

Forced warm air systems, especially in energy efficient homes, can move air from solar heated areas to other parts of the house, thus taking best advantage of passive solar gains, and increasing temperature uniformity.

Quality forced warm air systems must be designed by experienced professionals. Traditionally they have been installed by heating trades who relied on tried and true 'rules of thumb' which may not always be appropriate where accurate detailing is required. Rules of thumb developed years ago were okay when the standard furnace had less air moving capacity than today's more efficient appliances and when most houses were 1,200 square feet, rectangular bungalows with basements and uniform construction characteristics. This does not reflect today's wide range of architectural designs, structural, mechanical and construction specifications.

In order for a forced warm air heating system to deliver the right amount of warm air to every room in the home, a properly sized and sealed duct system for both supply air and return air must be installed. The ducts must return to the furnace the same amount of air that the furnace is delivering. If the return air system is undersized and/or improperly sealed, the furnace will create a negative pressure in some areas

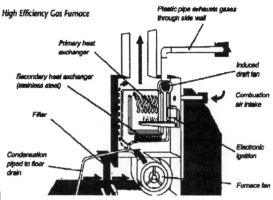

High Efficiency Gas Furnace

The pricing information reflects average prices on the south coast of BC in 1999. The square footage should include the total conditioned space (including heated basements). The numbers are only included to offer an indication of relative values of each system for an "average" home. Specific prices will vary from region to region.

7. Heating system types

of the house and affect the safe operation of itself and other fuel-fired appliances in the home. Today's more efficient furnaces move larger volumes of air than in the past. Ducts must be designed carefully to accommodate these larger air flows, otherwise it could create unwanted noise as undersized ducts are noisy.

Every fitting (registers, T connections, screens, etc.) adds resistance to air flow so the more complicated the layout, with many elbows and fittings, the greater the resistance to air flow. If the layout is not designed correctly, with proper fittings to reduce resistance to air flow, you get uneven air distribution depriving distant rooms of the heat they need.

Proprietary systems designed to use special small diameter ducts are available. However, these are sold as a whole packaged system by manufacturer trained suppliers.

Unfortunately, because in most municipalities there are no heating system installation inspections, many improperly designed and undersized duct systems are being installed with the new furnaces capable of moving larger quantities of air.

The system design must consider if cooling or air filtration are to be included. Filters add resistance to air movement, especially as they fill up with dust. The blower must be capable of moving air against this increased pressure. Cooling generally requires higher air flows than heating so the blower capacity and duct sizes may have to be increased, depending on the cooling requirement of the house.

More training courses are becoming available so tradespeople have practical tools available to them for furnace selection and duct sizing. Ask your local heating contractors' association, mechanical equipment wholesalers or utility if there are any residential heating system certification programs in your area. These programs include installer training and certification and sometimes third party inspections of the completed installation.

Forced Warm Air Systems

Advantages
- ☞ Moderate cost
- ☞ Variety of heat sources
- ☞ Generally low maintenance
- ☞ Easy to incorporate ventilation and cooling
- ☞ Allows for whole house air filtration
- ☞ Furniture layout not as restricted as with baseboard systems
- ☞ Humidity control can be added if needed
- ☞ Solar heat can be distributed by using the air circulation system

Disadvantages
- ☞ More difficult to zone
- ☞ Large volumes of space required to fit air ducts
- ☞ A poorly installed system can be a source of irritation, drafts and noise
- ☞ Flue gas spillage possible with many fuel fired furnaces if return air ducts are leaky

---

7. Heating system types

Baseboard Heating

Baseboard heaters, as the name implies, resemble oversized baseboards. Baseboard units are usually mounted along the exterior wall, preferably under a window, about ¾" off the floor. Generally, the output of a baseboard is dependent on its length. The bigger the heat output required, the longer the baseboard.

Electric Baseboard Heating

Electric baseboards are available in a wide range of sizes and outputs from 300 watts. Most are 500 watts or larger, increasing in 250 watt increments.

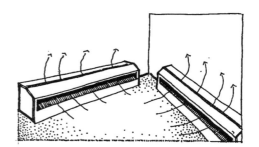

Heat Source
The heat source is a heating element that is an electrical resistance wire with fins to transfer heat to the air. Some baseboards contain a liquid heated by the electricity to release its heat at a lower temperature over a longer time.

Distribution
Heat is distributed by convection. A gentle floor-to-ceiling curtain of warm air blankets the outside walls and windows. The air flow is established naturally as the air is warmed by the heater. Some units provide part of their heat by radiation, but most new units have a radiation shield to reduce the radiant component.

Some baseboard units are available with small fans or blowers that help with air circulation. Fan forced units are usually used in small rooms with cabinets or built-in furniture where natural convection flows are difficult to establish or a conventional baseboard will not readily fit.

Controls
The electrical code requires electric baseboard heaters to be controlled by a thermostat in each room. As a result, each room is its own zone that can be set to its own temperature. The thermostat should always be mounted on an inside wall opposite from the heating unit. For good control, comfort and economy, low voltage wall mounted thermostats are recommended, but for best comfort use good quality diaphragm type line voltage or electronic line voltage thermostats.

The least costly baseboard units have a built-in line voltage thermostat thus avoiding the need to supply and install a separate thermostat. However, built-in thermostats are not as accurately controlled because they are located 4 inches above the floor, typically on an outside wall, and are affected by the heat generated within the baseboard itself. They can only provide thermal comfort conditions close to the floor near one end of the baseboard. It is not always easy to reach the built in controls to adjust the settings. Baseboards with built-in thermostats are not recommended for rooms requiring uniform heating comfort.

7. Heating system types

Capital Costs

Electric baseboard heating is the least expensive system to install. The approximate cost of an installed electric baseboard heating system is between $0.70 - $1.00 per square foot of house floor area.

Other Considerations

Electric baseboard heaters are popular because of their low initial cost and simple installation. They are often used for additions, where new rooms may be hard to tie into existing heating systems. They are also often used in seasonally occupied buildings, such as cottages, where low capital costs may be important considerations. However, they are always expensive to operate because of higher electrical energy costs.

As each room is its own zone, comfortable conditions for each room can be maintained if good quality controls are used. Because of the high operating temperatures (as high as 350°F [176°C] at the fins), the dust in the air flowing past the heater gets scorched and odours generated. Dust streaks above the baseboard form due to the air movement against the wall, as the dust particles are deposited on the wall..

Recessed wall heaters are mostly used in the toe space of cabinets (such as the kitchen and bathrooms). Recessed heaters entail greater costs because of the additional work involved with the framing of the recess and tend to be less effective in heating larger rooms.

Installation is handled by the electrical contractor. Usually only the better quality tradespeople have the training to do heating design and calculation.

Electric Baseboard Heating
Advantages
- Lowest initial cost
- Low maintenance
- Individual room control
- Wide variety of equipment sizes
- Good for additions or hard to heat areas
- No fuel to spill or leak
- No combustion gases
- Flexible layout possible

Disadvantages
- Expensive to operate if electric rates are high
- Takes up space as clearance is needed to allow for air flow
- Restricts furniture placement (furniture should not restrict air flows)
- Can get very hot
- Odours from scorched dust
- Dust leaves streak marks on the wall
- Ventilation must be provided separately
- Can generate a noise as the unit heats and cools

Hot Water (Hydronic) Baseboards

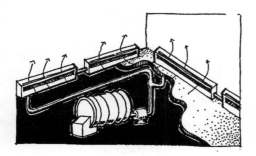

Hydronic baseboard systems are similar in appearance and function to electric baseboards except that the heat is provided by hot water supplied from a boiler or water heater. The thermal mass and lower temperature of the water in the piping tends to provide a more even heat distribution, reducing the sudden on-off temperature cycles of an electric baseboard.

Heat Source

The heat source is a central boiler or domestic hot water tank that heats water for delivery to the baseboards. Can use various fuel sources.

7. Heating system types

Distribution
Hot water is circulated through pipes to the baseboards, which contain a pipe with fins to transfer heat from the fins to the air. A gentle, floor-to-ceiling curtain of warm air blankets the outside walls and windows. The air flow is established naturally as the air is warmed by the heater.

Controls
Hydronic baseboards can be laid out so that each floor of the house is a single zone, operated by one low voltage thermostat, or individual rooms or areas of the house can be zoned with their own thermostat.

Capital Costs
The approximate cost of an installed hydronic baseboard system is about $1.75 - $2.50 per square foot of house floor area.

Other Considerations
Hydronic baseboard heaters provide a more even, lower temperature heat than electric baseboards because of the thermal mass in the water. The operating temperature of the water is usually 160 - 190°F (71-87°C). Because of the lower operating temperatures, less dust gets scorched and there are fewer dust streaks above the baseboard.

Installation is handled by plumbing contractors, but they are likely not to have the skills for heating system design.

A good idea is to have a separate baseboard zone for the bathrooms. This will provide continuous heat to the bathrooms, to keep them dryer, while the bedroom temperatures may be set back at night.

Hot Water (Hydronic) Baseboards

Advantages	Disadvantages
☞Can use boiler for domestic hot water also	☞Needs clearance to wall
☞Good zone control potential	☞Restricts furniture placement (furniture should not restrict air flows)
☞Uses less space as pipes are easily concealed	☞Dust leaves streak marks on the wall
☞Thermal mass of water provides a more even heat, providing better comfort	☞Can generate a noise as the unit heats and cools
☞Lower operating temperatures	☞Ventilation must be provided separately

---

Radiant Heating

Radiant heating is recognized for its comfort. Its principle has been known and valued for centuries. Ancient cliff dwellings were designed to allow the sun to heat buildings through window openings where the stone floors and walls absorbed the heat during the day and radiated it back into the room at night. Roman baths were designed with underfloor ducts that carried hot air to warm the floors that in turn radiated heat into the room. Medieval castles in central and eastern Europe had kitchen fires and ovens placed so the heat would also heat the brickwork to keep rooms above warm. Traditional Korean homes were designed with ducts in the ceiling that carried the heat from fires to warm the mass of the structure that in turn radiated back into the living areas.

7. Heating system types

Radiant systems work by heating surfaces, usually the ceiling or floor, so the heat radiates into the room, increasing the room's surface temperatures. Air temperatures can be kept lower (for equivalent comfort) than with other systems.

From the standpoint of ability to heat it does not matter whether the warm surface is the floor, walls or ceiling. The ceiling and floor are the most practical as the heat can be distributed from the largest surface area available. Wall heating panels are rarely used for practical considerations of damage if nails or other fixtures penetrate the wall. Several manufacturers make heated towel bars and decorative metal panels used mostly in bathrooms, but these are basically convectors.

Monitored results have shown that temperatures in radiant heated spaces are more even with less variation of temperatures between the floor and ceiling.

Manufacturers often claim that a radiant system is more "efficient" or economical to operate than a conventional forced warm air system. This is a difficult claim to prove. Radiant systems may have reduced operating costs because they are effectively zoned. In well insulated houses, thermostats may be set at 68°F rather than 70 or 72°F for an equivalent comfort level. Unfortunately many people keep thermostats for radiant heating systems set to maintain air temperatures the same as if they had forced warm air heating.

Radiant Ceiling Systems

Heat Source
The two most common radiant ceiling panels are electric foils or drywall panels that come fully assembled from the factory. Thin flat foils are enclosed in a protective plastic covering. These are attached to the ceiling joists, wired to the main electrical panel and covered with a surface material such as drywall. Drywall panels have heating wires embedded in the gypsum and are attached to the ceiling structure before the finished ceiling is installed.

Distribution
The heat is distributed by radiation from the ceiling as it is warmed by the radiant panels. The panels heat the ceiling drywall to surface temperatures up to 130°F (55°C) to radiate heat to the room below, much as the sun radiates its heat to the earth. Hydronic ceiling panels in homes are unusual.

Controls
The electrical panels are controlled by individual room thermostats. Diaphragm or electronic thermostat is recommended.

Costs
The approximate cost of an installed radiant ceiling heating system is about $1.50 - $2.00 per square foot of house floor area.

7. Heating system types

Other Considerations

There is a limit to how much heat can be supplied. The heat output is 35 - 100 BTU/Sq.Ft. (10 - 30 W/Sq.Ft.).

There have been problems with carbon-based ceiling radiant panels as they overheated, creating possibilities of a fire. Contact your local or provincial electrical safety branch for information. Approved products currently on the market use wires and are safe when installed according to manufacturers instructions and electrical code requirements. Some have been in use for more than 50 years. All will have a CSA or UL certification.

Higher levels of insulation must be installed in the ceiling above the panels, otherwise the warmer ceiling temperatures will increase heat loss from the building.

Radiant Ceiling Systems

Advantages
- ☞ Low maintenance
- ☞ Allows higher mean radiant temperatures and lower air temperatures
- ☞ Individual room control
- ☞ Modular panel sizes can be suited to the needs for each room
- ☞ Good for additions or hard to heat areas
- ☞ No fuel to spill or leak
- ☞ No combustion gases
- ☞ Does not take up space
- ☞ Invisible

Disadvantages
- ☞ Expensive to operate if electric rates are high
- ☞ Air filtration and ventilation must be provided separately
- ☞ Slower response time than non-radiant systems
- ☞ Can have excessive heat loss to an attic above unless high density rock wool insulation is used.

Radiant Floor Systems

In the 1940's hot water radiant systems became quite popular in some areas, most with metal pipes embedded in concrete. However, problems arose when the copper or iron pipe started to corrode and many systems leaked and caused water damage.

Significant advances have been made in recent years in the types and quality of radiant heating components.

Heat Source

In hydronic systems, a boiler is used to heat the water that circulates through in-floor piping. Heat output is determined by pipe spacing, water temperature and flow rate. In electric systems, heating panels or cables are placed into the floor, and heat output is determined by cable length, spacing and watt density (watts/square foot).

Distribution

A radiant floor system is similar to a ceiling system, but here the floor becomes the heating element. The most common floor heating system installations are hot water pipes or electric cables in a concrete slab-on-grade or embedded in a 1½" topping that acts as a thermal mass installed

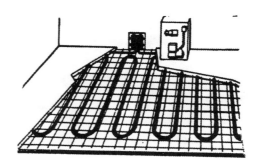

Floor radiant heating system layout. Can be pipes for warm water or electric cables.

7. Heating system types

on top of a wood floor. Sometimes the heating pipes will be attached below the wood subfloor with insulation and reflectors, but these have to be designed properly due to the insulating properties of the wood subfloor above, and more importantly, due to the carpet and thick underlay that may be installed, which has an even higher insulation value.

Controls

Electric heating system control must be done on a room by room basis, as with any other electrical heater. With hydronic systems, each floor or area of the house can be zoned. The minimum recommended zoning is to have the north side on a separate zone from the south side rooms that receive solar energy. In this way, north side rooms can be kept comfortable, while south side rooms are heated by the solar gains.

A better, more sophisticated control strategy is to have indoor and outdoor thermostats. As the exterior temperature changes, the outdoor thermostat can start the system before the indoor control senses a need for heat.

Costs

The approximate cost of an installed radiant hot water floor heating system is about $3.00 - $5.50 per square foot of house floor area (electric cable is about $2.00 - $4.00). The upper range includes the cost of thermal mass that should be a part of every floor radiant heating system.

Other considerations

Today new oxygen-barriered plastic pipe (PEX) materials prevent oxygen from permeating the pipe walls and getting into the water. Oxygen rich circulating water will speed corrosion of some steel components in the boiler.

Radiant floor systems respond slowly to rapid changes in heating needs. Depending on the amount of thermal mass, it may take longer to raise the temperature, whether light weight concrete is used or not. This can be a concern during fall and spring when there are large outdoor temperature fluctuations. (In my home, a well-insulated slab-on-grade structure, I have found it takes about two to three hours to raise the temperature 1°C on a fall day.) To minimize this problem indoor/outdoor temperature controls can be used.

There is a potential of overheating well-insulated houses in mild weather conditions, especially at times of high direct solar gains (such as in the morning as the sun rises) and if there is inadequate thermal mass in the house to absorb the heat. Fortunately radiant systems are easy to zone, so a proper zone layout along with careful control can reduce the overheating problem by anticipating the possibility of having these conditions.

The slow response is especially noticeable when there is a need to reduce heat, as can happen on a sunny day when solar gains can raise the indoor air temperature quickly. If there is a large thermal mass in the house, the overheating will not be as pronounced.

Electric floor radiant heating panels by Nuheat. They can be used for renovation applications as well as new construction.

Not only does the thermal mass provide a more even temperature, but the heat storage capacity of the mass is useful in areas subject to power outages as the slab can store energy, retaining its heat for a long time. With concrete slabs-on-grade, the entire concrete floor area must be well insulated underneath the slab and along the perimeter.

Floor radiant systems operate at low surface temperatures of up to 85°F (29°C), which is the limit that a human body can tolerate on an ongoing basis.

A radiant floor system can deliver up to 30 - 35 BTU per square foot per hour. This should be enough for most rooms in most climates. However, in room with a large heat loss, such as a poorly insulated living room with a large wall of glass, there may be a problem unless supplementary heat is provided. More heat can't be supplied by just raising the temperature of the floor surface as it will put the floor above the comfort level. Depending on the design, it may be possible to place extra heating pipes spaced more closely near the perimeter of the room, in front of the large glass areas.

The type of floor finish (its thickness and insulating value) must be considered when designing the system, as finished flooring materials can be an insulator that restricts heat flow.

The short-term temperature fluctuations that characterize many heating systems in poorly insulated houses are not as likely to be seen with radiant systems, especially if there is adequate thermal mass.

Radiant floor system design is more sophisticated than other heating system types, so most major component manufacturers have developed detailed installation manuals and design tools for the trades who install their products. Many wholesalers offer design services for their trade customers, and in some local jurisdictions building inspectors require a system design and a sign-off by the installing contractor.

Radiant Floor systems

Advantages
- ☞High comfort
- ☞Low operating temperature
- ☞No drafts
- ☞Thermal mass evens out temperature fluctuations
- ☞Good zoning potential
- ☞Invisible completely hidden - easy furniture layout
- ☞Low temperature gradient within a room
- ☞Warm floors
- ☞Silent
- ☞Well suited to bathrooms or special use areas with hard floor finishes.

Disadvantages
- ☞Higher initial cost
- ☞Slow to respond during sunny fall/spring days
- ☞Possible overheating at some times of the year
- ☞Night setbacks not practical in most situations
- ☞Leaks are rare, but expensive to repair in a slab if one develops
- ☞Ventilation must be done separately
- ☞Extra support needed for weight of thermal mass topping on a wood floor

---

7. Heating system types

Combination (Combo) Systems

Every house needs hot water for domestic use. The usual practice has been to install separate water and space heating systems. The water heater provides hot water year round, but in practice it sits idle for about 22 hours every day. Similarly, the furnace is idle whenever the weather is warm.

In today's energy efficient houses, the total heat load is quite small, so combining the heat source for both heating and hot water enables the use of a single, higher efficiency heat source to do double duty. These systems are commonly called combo or combination systems.

Heat Source

A boiler or domestic hot water heater is usually the heat source. The heated water is circulated by a pump to the distribution system.

Distribution

Combination systems allow a mixture of distribution options. Radiant floor heat can be used in some areas, and others can be heated by forced warm air or hot water baseboards. For example, radiant floor heating for the bathrooms and kitchen, forced warm air to the bedrooms and living areas, and a baseboard could heat the basement workshop.

Many combo systems distribute heat to the house by a forced warm air distribution system using a fan-coil (essentially a radiator with a fan) that pushes air past the water coil. The ductwork and system layout is similar to that of a regular forced warm air furnace. The fan-coil units are smaller than a furnace, and depending on the size of the house, several fan-coil units may be used in the house. They could be mounted above closets, stairways, etc., the main limitation being the space needed to house properly sized ducts.

Combination systems can also be used for hydronic heating systems, such as baseboard or floor radiant. In those cases the heating loop is designed and installed as any conventional baseboard or radiant floor hot water heating system.

Controls

The control is a low voltage thermostat and the strategy matches the type of heat distribution (forced warm air or hot water).

Costs

The approximate cost of a combo heating system is about $2.00 - $4.00 per square foot of house area.

Other considerations

Some manufacturers have packaged system units. Installers of combo systems must be familiar with sheet metal and also plumbing.

Although combination heating systems are a recent development, they are acceptable by all codes if installed according to design and sizing guidelines (but it is worth confirming with the local building inspector). Because the heater is doing double duty, the system must be sized correctly to handle water and space heating needs.

Combination heating system with forced warm air heating.

Lennox Industries' Completeheat packaged combo system

Radiant floor heating systems are designed so as not to circulate potable water through the floor. They use an intermediate heat exchanger to keep the potable water separate from the heating loop. Industry guidelines have been developed to deal with concerns regarding the possible compromise of health and safety relating to bacterial infection.

It is estimated that this type of system has been used in about one million dwellings in the United States over the past twenty years, and up to 60,000 in Ontario alone over the last ten.

Combination (Combo) Systems

Advantages
☞ Uses only one water heater or boiler for the heat source
☞ Only one combustion gas vent is needed if unit is fuel fired
☞ A fan-coil unit can be easier to install than a conventional furnace and can be located in tight or difficult to reach areas
☞ May require less maintenance
☞ Can be integrated with ventilation system

Disadvantages
☞ Generally a higher initial cost
☞ Require knowledgeable technicians for proper design and installation
☞ Best with energy efficient construction
☞ Generally not very efficient if a conventional hot water tank is used

---

Unitary Space Heaters

Unitary systems are self contained heating appliances intended for installation in the space to be heated and not connected to other spaces by ducts or pipes. The heating unit may be a register, baseboard, panel, fireplace or stove. Energy is provided directly to and from each heater.

Unitary heaters are often used for additions to an existing home where providing heat using the existing heating system is difficult because extending the distribution system is impossible or the heating system does not have enough capacity. In new homes, unitary heaters may not be appropriate except for special use areas (e.g., a workshop, hobby room, or an "in-law suite") remote from the main portion of the house, or where an area is to be totally separated.

Heat Source
Can be electric or non-electric combustion heat sources.

Recently a variety of sealed combustion gas fired unitary heaters have been developed. These include baseboard and wall mounted units that can be installed with thermostats. Direct vent natural gas fireplaces are used to provide space heating in many apartments and small homes.

Gas and oil unitary space heaters require fuel to be piped to the unit and a flue vent installed. In gas direct vent heaters, the combustion process is isolated from the interior of the house. The burners, pilot lights, combustion chamber and all flue gas passages are isolated from the space it is heating. The flue goes through the wall to the outside, and the combustion air inlet extends through the same wall opening.

From a healthy indoor environment perspective, it is always preferable to rely on direct vented, sealed combustion appliances.

7. Heating system types

Distribution
Heat is distributed mainly by fan forced convection and radiation directly from the heating unit.

Controls
Like an electric baseboard, some incremental space heaters come with a built-in thermostat but these will not be as effective as a separate wall mounted thermostat.

Cost
Because of the wide variety of heaters available, it is not possible to generalise the cost of incremental heaters. Electric heaters cost from $100 per unit; direct vent gas baseboards $350 or more.

Unitary Space Heaters
Advantages
☞Individual room control provides convenience
☞Often treated as supplementary heat source
☞Some space saving as furnace room can be eliminated
☞Wide selection of heater types
☞Good for additions or hard to heat areas

Disadvantages
☞Electric units expensive to operate where electric rates are high
☞Fuel fired units need piped source of fuel
☞Needs clearance to wall
☞Restricts furniture placement (furniture should not restrict air flows)
☞Air filtration not available
☞Ventilation must be provided separately

Gas Fireplaces

Gas fireplaces have become very popular in recent years. They cater to our desire for comfort and convenience because they are clean burning and instantly "on" while providing the visual enchantment of a fireplace.

One kind of gas fireplace is the traditional open fireplace that uses a ceramic log with a gas burner. This has a standing pilot light and is vented up a flue much like a traditional fireplace. When the fireplace is off, it contributes to heat loss because the flue must remain open to allow the venting of the pilot light gases. Open gas fireplaces cannot be considered space heaters.

A second type of gas fireplace is the direct vented unit. This contains the gas combustion in a sealed chamber behind glass so you still have the full visual impact of the flame and the radiant heat of the fire. Combustion air is brought in from the outside and combustion gases are vented through the back or top depending on the unit design, but does not affect the interior of the house.

Heat Source
Natural gas or propane flame.

Distribution
Heat is distributed mainly by radiation and some convection. Some models have fans to enhance convection air flows.

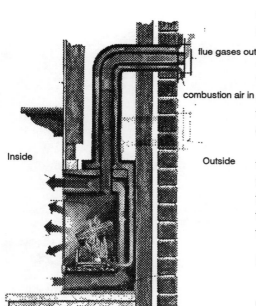

flue gases out

combustion air in

Inside

Outside

Cut-away through direct vent fireplace.

Controls

Most gas fireplaces have a wall mounted on/off switch to turn on the flame. Some can be hooked up to a thermostat to operate automatically as a space heater.

Cost

The cost can vary based on unit design, size and mantelpiece design and trim. A typical budget price is $2,000-2,500.

Other considerations

Some gas fireplaces have no standing pilot flame, but use a manual, non-electric "piezo" igniter.

Direct vent units are reasonably efficient and can be used to provide principal space heating for a larger area.

An efficiency rating standard is under development by the Canadian Gas Association. Most manufacturers have test results based on a draft version of the standard.

Gas Fireplaces

Advantages	Disadvantages
☞Quiet except if there is a fan	☞Needs larger room to provide clearance in front
☞Visually appealing - focus of room	☞Heat distribution through the house can be challenging
☞Individual room control provides convenience	☞Restricts furniture placement
☞Can be principal or supplementary heat source for a room or area	☞Not suited to all rooms
☞Wide selection of designs	☞There are limits to the distance flue gases can be vented

---

Wood Fireplaces

Fireplaces and woodstoves have a long history. Wood is, after all, the oldest fuel mankind has used and fire has an emotional appeal.

Heat source

Wood.

Distribution

Heat is distributed mainly by radiation and some convection. Some manufactured fireplace units have fans to enhance convection air flows. Ducted circulation to an adjoining room is possible.

Controls

This is primarily a manual system. The home owner must load the firebox and stoke the fire to generate any heat.

Other considerations

May not be appropriate for use in urban areas due to fuel wood supply and concerns about air pollution.

Heat content of wood varies depending on species and moisture content.

7. Heating system types

Inadequate supply of air to a fireplace or stove can cause the fire to meet its air requirements by sucking air from other combustion appliance flues. If this happens, dangerous flue gases may spill into the house. Glass doors may limit spillage, and when used properly with combustion air, will prevent spillage.

Usually, houses can satisfy combustion air requirements (supplied by leakage) without a make-up air system, provided large exhaust fans are not installed. Except at start up, to get a draft established, even tightly sealed houses have enough natural leakage to supply combustion air to controlled wood burning appliances.

The traditional open English fireplace without doors is probably the most inefficient design ever devised and should not be considered as an effective heating system. It removes much more heated air from the house than is required for combustion. Even though they are fitted with a damper that should be closed when not in operation, the dampers warp and seldom have a sufficiently tight fit to be effective to stop heated indoor air from escaping up the flue when not in use.

Traditional masonry fireplaces actually are not conducive to successful venting. They are very vulnerable to combustion spillage.

Chimneys should always be located inside the heated envelope of the house (rather than on an outside wall), penetrating only at or near the highest portion of the roof. This way the chimney remains warm through most of its length, enhancing the draft, reducing the chances of flue gas spillage.

Masonry chimneys have thermal storage capacity, which creates a thermal momentum making it somewhat resistant to spillage during the fire tail-out phase when the fire is dying (especially if the chimney is inside the house rather than outside as in many houses). An interior chimney radiates heat back into the house, rather than outside, enhancing the overall efficiency of the fire.

There is a significant human factor in wood burning that affects safety. Users allow the fire to smoulder, a condition that promotes dangerous gas formation, and potential spillage of combustion gases (including carbon monoxide) into the house.

New manufactured hearth products (wood stoves, gas fireplaces, masonry stoves) are tested to meet performance and emissions criteria. High efficiency wood stoves tested to meet US Environmental Protection Agency (EPA) emission standards reduce air pollution and wood consumption.

Wood Fireplaces
Advantages
- ☞Visually appealing
- ☞Secure in case of a power outage
- ☞Wood is a renewable fuel
- ☞Moderate installation cost
- ☞Gives homeowner lots of exercise
- ☞Temperature control is simple

Disadvantages
- ☞High maintenance (cleaning, chimney sweeping)
- ☞High temperature gradient within room
- ☞Heat distribution through the house can be challenging
- ☞Generates odours, smoke, ashes, creosote
- ☞High interior pollution, mess, dust, bugs
- ☞Can be a fire hazard
- ☞Requires wood shed, tools, etc.
- ☞Time consuming for the homeowner

7. Heating system types

Wood Stoves

When we think of wood stoves, we think of pioneers' cook stoves and radiant wood stoves that have regained popularity in recent years.

Heat Source
Wood

Distribution
Heat is distributed mainly by radiation and some convection directly from the unit.

Controls
This is a manual system. The home owner must load the firebox and stoke the fire to generate heat.

Other considerations
Wood heating appliances must be installed precisely to manufacturers' specifications and according to appropriate codes and standards. Because of fire hazard, many jurisdictions have special permit and inspection requirements for wood heater installations. The stove must be sized correctly and placed in an appropriate location with specified minimum clearances.

Chimneys must be carefully and regularly cleaned.

Many insurance companies charge a premium for wood heated homes. (Some may not insure a wood heated home).

Chimneys should always be inside the heated envelope of the house, penetrating only at or near the highest portion of the roof. This way the chimney remains warm through most of its length, enhancing the draft, reducing the chances of flue gas spillage.

Masonry chimneys have thermal storage capacity, which creates a thermal momentum making it somewhat resistant to spillage during the fire tail-out phase when the fire is dying (especially if the chimney is inside the house rather than outside as in many older houses).

In some parts of northern Europe, if wood heating is used, a permanent ladder must be attached to the roof to provide access to the chimney for easy cleaning. This is not commonly done in Canada, but is an idea that should be considered if wood is the fuel of choice.

Wood may not be appropriate in urban areas due to fuel wood supply and concerns about air pollution.

Wood Stoves	Disadvantages
Advantages	☞High maintenance (cleaning, chimney sweeping)
☞Visually appealing	☞High surface temperature depending on material and design
☞Secure in case of a power outage	☞High temperature gradient within room
☞Wood is a renewable fuel	☞Heat distribution through the house can be challenging
☞Moderate installation cost	☞Generates odours, smoke, ashes, creosote
☞Gives homeowner lots of exercise	☞High interior pollution, mess, dust, bugs
☞Temperature control is simple	☞Can be a fire hazard
☞Low operating costs	☞May increase home insurance costs
	☞Requires wood shed, tools, etc.
	☞Time consuming for the homeowner

7. Heating system types

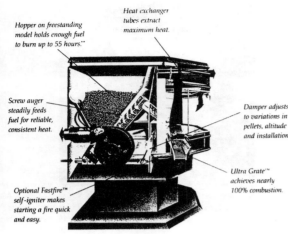

Hopper on freestanding model holds enough fuel to burn up to 55 hours.''

Heat exchanger tubes extract maximum heat.

Screw auger steadily feeds fuel for reliable, consistent heat.

Damper adjusts to variations in pellets, altitude and installation.

Ultra Grate'" achieves nearly 100% combustion.

Optional Fastfire™ self-igniter makes starting a fire quick and easy.

Pellet stoves

Pellet stoves are a variation on the wood stove but they rely on wood pellets for fuel. The pellets are manufactured from wood waste and what is otherwise considered low grade wood pressed into small pellets. Pellets are reasonably clean, so the dirt and dust normally associated with wood is not present. Most pellet stoves have automatic feeders, shifting the pellets to the fire, thus reducing the amount of manual stoking required.

While the manufacture of pellets is a simple, low-technology process, pellets may not be available everywhere. If you are considering a pellet stove, try to ensure there are two or more sources of supply in the area, otherwise you might find yourself with a supply problem in the event the one supplier goes out of business or stops handling pellets.

Masonry Heaters

Masonry heaters are a cross between a wood stove and a fireplace. They are intended to burn the fuel very fast at high temperatures for maximum combustion efficiency. The high thermal mass of the unit stores the heat. They are also known as contra-flow fireplaces, Russian, Finnish and German Kachelofen or European tile stoves. Many are available as prefabricated kits and have US EPA ratings.

Tile stoves are designed with a series of baffled chambers through which exhaust gasses and smoke pass. The chimney connection is made at the back or side of the unit. Smoke and flue gases exit here after they have moved through the baffles. These units can achieve efficiencies of up to 80%.

Heat Source
Wood

Distribution
Heat is distributed mainly by radiation and some convection.

Controls
This is a manual system. The home owner must load the firebox and stoke the fire to generate any heat.

Cost
Prefabricated core units typically start at around $4,000. An installed unit will probably cost $9,000 or more when all installation and finishing costs are included.

Other considerations
Combustion can be efficient and clean because the hot fire recommended allows a more complete combustion to take place, so the chimney remains cleaner.

Masonry heaters absorb considerable amounts of heat, reducing the potential of overheating a house.

Installation requires a competent mason.

Wood may not be appropriate in urban areas due to fuel wood supply and concerns about air pollution.

7. Heating system types

Masonry Heaters

Advantages	Disadvantages
☞Low surface temperatures	☞Heat distribution to other rooms may be challenging
☞Quiet	☞Heavy (needs a foundation)
☞Not reliant on electric power	☞High interior pollution, mess, dirt, dust, and bugs
☞Aesthetically appealing and cosy	☞Requires considerable maintenance (cleaning, chimney sweeping, etc.)
☞Stores solar heat	☞High installation cost
☞Low external pollution	☞Higher fire insurance
☞Efficient, low wood consumption in comparison to all other wood heaters	
☞Low fire hazard	

Heat Pumps

Heat pumps of various types have been used for many years. We may not recognize them as such, because they are used to keep our food cool rather than provide heat. They are also used for heating, cooling, dehumidification or domestic water heating.

A heat pump can discharge more heat than the energy supplied to it through the transfer of heat using a refrigerant fluid such as freon or HCFC. For 1 kWh of energy, the unit can deliver the equivalent of 2 or 3 kWh of heat.

Heat pump cycles can be reversed, so they can provide summer cooling as well as winter heating.

Heat pumps can provide summer cooling as well as winter heating.

Heat Source

The heat source is the compressor run by electricity. Heat may be drawn from the ground, a water body, ambient air, and ventilation air. When the air temperature falls below freezing, air systems use electricity as back-up, making the air source heat pump less desirable in areas with low winter temperatures.

Distribution

Central heat pumps are commonly attached to forced warm air heating distribution systems, but radiant floor hot water (hydronic) distribution systems can also be used.

Controls

Standard low voltage thermostatic control as for forced warm air systems or heating/cooling thermostats when cooling is to be provided.

Costs

The approximate cost of a heat pump heating system is about $4.00 - $8.00 per square foot of heated floor area.

If heat pumps are being considered, the design of the house and careful calculation of its heating and cooling loads are important. Unlike other heating equipment (for gas, oil, propane or electricity), heat pump equipment capacity does significantly affect system cost. The cost of

7. Heating system types

upgrades to house insulation levels and window glass can be easily offset by reductions in the size of the heat pumps required, which will also mean lower operating costs.

Other considerations

Heat pumps require more careful maintenance than other heating systems to remain at peak operating capacity.

Where there is no cooling load, the heat pump has lower overall savings and capital costs are still relatively high. In most areas of North America, typical operating costs for heat pump heating/cooling systems are about half those of electrical heating.

Successful installations require proper sizing, good duct systems, a quality control system, and a skilful installer. The operating temperatures of heat pumps are lower than for combustion or electric appliances. Cooler air temperatures require larger sized ducts for forced warm air systems to maintain comfort and avoid drafts.

With air-to-air heat pumps, at outdoor temperatures below freezing, the unit effectively switches to operating as a resistance heater. That is why so many central air conditioners are linked to conventional fuel fired furnaces and designed for cooling only.

Geothermal heat pumps are the highest efficiency heat pump. Because below ground temperatures remain above freezing, a coil in the ground will always provide a source of heat to the heat pump in the heating season, and a heat sink in the summer to accept excess heat from the house. Large bodies of water, such as lakes or the ocean can also be used as the source of heat.

Heat Pumps
Advantages
- ☞Energy source is solar energy from the air or solar heated earth
- ☞Low external pollution
- ☞Very efficient when compared with electric furnace.
- ☞Can be reversed to provide cooling and dehumidification

Disadvantages
- ☞Compressor units can be noisy
- ☞High installation cost
- ☞Ground source heat pumps require space for placement of coils
- ☞Often not cost efffective for small energy efficient houses
- ☞Requires competent system design and proper installation
- ☞Regular onging maintenance is required
- ☞Most units are still using ozone depleting HCFC's
- ☞Larger ducts are required for forced warm air systems

Solar Energy

The sun is the most environmentally friendly energy source available. Solar energy can be designed to provide a substantial portion of a home's space heating needs. Passive solar energy can contribute 30 to 50% if not more (depending on house design and lifestyle patterns).

Heat source

Two principal approaches are used to harness the sun's energy: active systems and passive systems.

7. Heating system types

Active solar systems consist of solar collector panels with separate heat storage placed at a distance from the collectors. In their simplest form, a fluid is circulated through a collector designed to absorb solar radiation and take the heat to a storage tank.

Passive solar systems are much simpler as the design of the house is adjusted to take full advantage of solar energy. The house itself becomes both the energy collector and storage system. Windows (especially south and southwest facing) are the principal collectors of solar radiation. The mass of the house absorbs and stores the heat. In well-insulated energy efficient homes, passive solar can handle a significant portion of space heating needs.

Distribution
Radiant and convective heat transfer from the heated thermal mass. Direct sunlight raises the air temperature in south facing rooms.

Controls
Passive controls include the elements of the house's design. Roof overhangs and louvres can control solar heat gains on a seasonal basis. Manual and automatic blinds and awnings can also provide control over solar gains.

Costs
When considered at the design stage, passive solar systems do not add any additional cost to the house.

Active systems can be more expensive, depending on system design and size.

Other considerations
Experience over the past twenty years has shown that active systems are appropriate for water heating, but not usually cost effective for space heating because well built, energy efficient houses have a very small heat load.

Active solar systems that provide 100% of a house's domestic hot water needs have been proven to be technically feasible, although they tend to be expensive at most northern locations. The typical balance point is sixty percent of annual needs.

A south facing greenhouse or solarium can provide a significant amount of heat. It should be closed off from the heated space at night during cold weather. A solarium that is just a glazed portion of the living space, without a separation, will not be a net contributor of heat.

Solar Energy
Advantages:
- ☞No noise
- ☞No odours
- ☞No external pollution
- ☞An infinite fuel source
- ☞Low annual cost
- ☞Aesthetically pleasant

Disadvantages:
- ☞Difficult to regulate heat distribution
- ☞High temperature swings are possible, so there may be overheating in spring and fall due to a low sun angle
- ☞Excessive sun may fade fabrics
- ☞May not provide all the heat required

8. Domestic hot water

Domestic water heaters may be used for heating the house as well as providing hot water. Main types of water heaters are described.

Domestic hot water heaters are designed to provide hot water for bathing, laundry and dishwashing. Energy consumption for water heating averages between 35 - 50% of total household energy use. In an energy efficient home, more energy may be used for domestic hot water than for space heating. The difference is that space heating is only needed during cold weather, while hot water needs are year round. Properly sized, water heaters can be used to provide space heat as well.

Domestic water heaters can be grouped into several categories: storage tank heaters, instantaneous heaters, indirect water heaters, boilers, and solar heaters.

Storage Tank Heaters

Thirty and forty gallon storage tank water heaters are the most commonly used heaters in residential construction. Large quantities of water can be provided over short periods due to the amount of hot water stored in the insulated tank. Depending on the water quality, most water tank heaters can have a reliable life span of 5 to 12 years.

The heating element is inserted in the tank (if electric) or at the bottom of the tank (if gas). There will be some energy loss through the tank walls, as the water is maintained at the designated temperature. However, the better insulated the tank is, the lower the standby heat loss will be. The heat loss contributes to space heating as the heat is lost into the house during the winter. However, in warm weather and summer, when there is no call for heat, the heat loss can contribute to overheating.

The efficiency of conventional gas fired water heaters is low... power vented and direct vent units are better.

With a seasonal efficiency of about 45%, the overall efficiency of conventional gas fired water heaters is low. Power vented and direct vent units are more efficient (at around 58%) and are now widely available. Unlike conventional units, power vented or direct vent units use a small fan to exhaust combustion products and do not require vertical chimneys and flues, but can be vented outside through the wall. The direct vented heaters draw combustion air and exhaust directly through a vent in the outside wall, through a single opening.

It is worth mentioning that there is a considerable amount of moisture in the flue gases so that in cold weather the exhaust can generate significant steam clouds at the vent outside. This leads to condensation and considerable ice formation, which can be objectionable if there is an adjoining house in close promixity to a vent outlet placed on the side of the house. When the water heater is used only to provide hot water, the firing element is on for short periods, so steam and ice formation may not be significant. However, when it also provides space heating, as in a combo heating system, the unit will be fired for longer periods and the steam and ice will be noticeable, so location of the vent should be considered carefully.

High efficiency gas water heaters with efficiencies of 86-94% are now available. The heat exchanger, controls and corrosion resistant materials required for the high efficiency equipment means that they are more expensive than the direct vent or power vent models. If you have a high year round demand for hot water, it is worth considering the high efficiency equipment.

Instantaneous Heaters

Instantaneous water heaters, also called tankless water heaters, heat water only as required. These are commonly used in Europe and other parts of the world. A large heating element, typically natural gas, provides a continuous supply of hot water when water passes through the heater. These units are suitable to use where hot water demand is small or intermittent. Although they are very efficient, the units are more expensive than storage type heaters.

Instantaneous heaters operate only when there is a flow of water through the heater. They are designed to heat a small flow of water through a large temperature increase (ground water [city mains] temperatures are typically 40 - 45 °F while hot water temperatures are around 130 - 140 °F). A heating system operates at hotter temperatures (160 - 200 °F) so there is a potential for having boiling water in the system. This can be avoided, but requires more careful design and control valves which add to an already high equipment cost. That is why an instanteneous heater must be connected to a storage tank when used for space heating. The tank then is the reservoir from which the heating system draws its heat when heat is required.

Indirect Water Heaters

Indirect water heaters use a separate boiler (whose primary purpose is as a heat source for the hot water space heating) to provide the heat to water that is then stored in an insulated storage tank. These systems often have higher capacities than conventional storage tank type heaters. Well insulated tanks may have a lower standby loss, and high recovery rates as they are connected to boilers with a greater heating capacity than an equivalent hot water tank.

Solar Water Heaters

Solar water heating is an alternative to conventional water heating systems. Solar water heating technology is well understood and is commercially available. In Canada, because of geography, the solar energy available peaks in the summer and is at a minimum in winter.

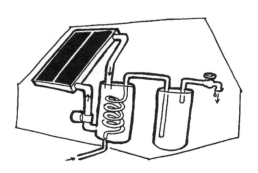

That is why most solar water heating systems are designed to preheat city or well water before it enters the heater. This way solar hot water can provide about 40-60% of annual hot water needs.

In summertime-only applications (such as at summer cottages) solar energy can provide 100% of domestic water needs. Solar water heating is well suited for use where hot water demands peak in summer and where electricity or propane are the only fuel sources available.

Typical domestic hot water preheating systems installed in British Columbia cost about $1,600.-2,000.

Water Heaters and Space Heating

In combination systems the water heater capacity and operating temperatures must be sized so there is enough heat to meet normal hot water needs, and heat the house.

When combination systems are considered, the decision on the kind of water heater to use is based on system size and operating temperatures. The home's heat loss must be known, so that the space heating can be sized properly. The heater must be big enough to meet both the normal hot water needs, and to meet the space heating load on the coldest winter day. To even out variations in domestic hot water and space heat needs, a storage tank is used. A storage tank is also important to maximize the efficiency of wood or oil burners, which must burn longer (than natural gas) to achieve maximum efficiency.

Operating temperatures of the heating system must be taken into account. Because domestic hot water is the major water user, for safety reasons, the temperature should not exceed normal water temperatures. The normal recommendation for hot water is a maximum of 140 °F (60 °C). Even at these temperatures there is a danger of burns to the body, so hotter temperatures increase the danger. Some systems may be designed with temperature regulating valves, so that water going to the kitchen and bathroom does not exceed a preset maximum.

If a forced warm air heating system is chosen, it must be designed for the lower temperatures available from the hot water tank (compared with a standard furnace, where the air temperature is much higher at the furnace).

9. Ventilation Systems

Ventilation is usually designed and installed along with heating systems. An effective ventilation system is key to maintaining good indoor air quality.

A home where the indoor environment feels stuffy and smelly when you enter it is a home with insufficient ventilation. Such conditions are unhealthy for many people, but can easily be corrected. An effective ventilation system is the key. Unfortunately, the understanding and design of ventilation systems is a new idea for most of the construction industry. Many builders, mechanical contractors and homeowners are still confused about the purpose and operation of ventilation systems because for many people ventilation seems to work against the heating system.

Air circulation through the house is not ventilation. To maintain healthy indoor air quality, the interior air must be continuously exchanged with the exterior to remove pollutants generated inside. Construction methods and details used today mean that mechanical ventilation must be provided during the heating season. Just opening a window and leaving ventilation to chance does not provide the effective ventilation most people think it does.

Air movement in the house is not ventilation. For healthy indoor air quality, interior pollutants must be removed continuously.

Opening a window does not provide the effective ventilation most people think it does.

Indoor Air Quality

In the past, indoor air quality was thought to have been maintained by random air leakage through openings in the building envelope. Current construction practices and the upgrading of existing housing have created better insulated, well-sealed buildings. This improves home comfort and reduces fuel bills. Air leakage, or raw uncontrolled air exchange, cannot be relied on for effective ventilation today.

However, reduced air leakage can cause new problems. We now recognize that indoor air can contain health compromising levels of contaminants as humidity and household odours become trapped inside. That is why mechanical ventilation systems are now required by the National Building Code.

While indoor air pollution is a general problem for everyone, there is a small but growing number of persons who are sensitive to common chemicals in our environment and very low levels of mould and mould spores. This sensitivity may result in seemingly unrelated allergic reactions such as eye irritation, dry throat, headaches, fatigue, coughing, sinus congestion, skin irritation, and shortness of breath. Often these people will describe the problem as excessive dryness or dust as they try to describe the cause of their problems. We have no words that can easily describe continual low level pollutant problems in our homes.

In addition, the ventilation system may deal with specific requirements inside the home such as removing pollutants from a home painting studio, hairdressing salon, automotive/woodworking shop and other special needs. The requirements of people with special sensitivities, such as chemical allergies, would fall into a special category as the ventilation rates necessary for these people to live comfortably may be much higher than normal.

Air leakage (natural air exchange) cannot be relied on for effective ventilation.

Seemingly unrelated allergic reactions such as eye irritation, dry throat, headaches, fatigue, coughing, sinus congestion, skin irritation, and shortness of breath may be symptoms of poor indoor air quality and lack of adequate ventilation.

9. Ventilation Systems

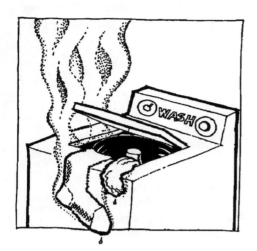

A good ventilation system will exhaust pollutants and replace the spent air with fresh air.

Purpose of a Ventilation System

The primary objective of ventilation is to deal with the basic needs of the occupants. Ventilation handles the moisture, odours and carbon dioxide generated by the occupants of the house. The installed capacity of the ventilation system should meet the home's designed occupancy. A family with a full time homemaker, four small children and several pets in a small house will generate more pollutants and require more fresh air than a couple working outside the house with no children or pets in a large home. The ventilation system should allow some control of air-flows to satisfy a range of needs, but have the overall capacity to meet the total occupancy needs for which the house is designed.

A good ventilation system will exhaust air containing pollutants generated by people and their activities to the outdoors and replace the spent air with fresh air. It must distribute the air evenly throughout the house, mixing or diffusing it to avoid discomfort. Climate, heating system, quality and safety of combustion appliances and home design will all affect the ventilation system design.

Moisture Control

Moisture generated by the occupants or brought into the house from the exterior can be a problem. Interior moisture is occupant generated by normal household functions such as bathing, cooking, occupants (because of skin evaporation and breathing), pets, and indoor plants. The moisture generated by these sources should be removed by the ventilation system.

Moisture by itself is not the pollutant, but rather the microbes and biological agents that thrive and multiply in high humidity conditions are. The optimum relative humidity levels for human comfort and reduction of respiratory ailments are 40-60%. High relative humidity levels are a greater concern than lower humidities.

Other sources of moisture in a house, which can often be many times that of occupant generated moisture, include ground water (especially if there is no moisture barrier below the basement floor or if capillary action draws water up from a wet footing), leaks through walls or roof, and wet fire wood drying inside or clothes dryers vented indoors. All these must be dealt directly by eliminating the moisture source, rather than relying on dehumidification by ventilation.

Ventilation Effectiveness

What is a safe, healthy, ventilation system design? All ventilation systems use fans to move air. The best will be silent, create no drafts, leave no odours, use little energy, and thus be virtually transparent to the homeowner. The better the system, the less likely you will know it is installed and working. Systems using lower cost equipment in a poor layout generally give themselves away through noise or ineffectiveness.

The best ventilation system is silent, creates no drafts, leaves no odours, uses little energy, and is invisible to the homeowner.

9. Ventilation Systems

One of our common misconceptions is that all ventilation strategies are equally effective. We are interested in the efficiency of the equipment but often give little thought to the effectiveness of the total system. Effectiveness of the system is important in maintaining the health of you and your home. Like heating systems, installation labour makes up ⅔ to ¾ of the total installed ventilation system cost, so it plays a very important role in whether the system operates satisfactorily. Comparing the energy efficiency of equipment options should be done only after you have determined that the proposed system will be effective for your needs.

Energy efficiency of equipment should only be considered after you have decided the system is effective for your needs.

Effective ventilation must thoroughly but slowly "wash" air through the whole occupied space. Ventilation must do this with a minimum of fresh outdoor air, so that the house is not over ventilated which will over dry the house and be overly wasteful of energy. To be effective, a ventilation system must control condensation and keep the house fresh. A symptom of excessive ventilation and a leaky building envelope is indoor air that is uncomfortably dry in winter and high heating bills. The layout and workmanship of an installation determine the effectiveness and efficiency of the system much more than the rated efficiency of the equipment itself.

System layout and workmanship determines the effectiveness and efficiency of a ventilation system.

A widespread belief persists that ventilation can control all indoor air pollutants. This is only partially true. Eliminating a pollutant at its source is far easier, more effective, and generally less expensive than relying on diluting the same pollutant with ventilation. Removing pollutants using dilution ventilation after the fact is not completely effective and wasteful of energy.

There are four strategies to control indoor air pollution, one for each of four very different types of contaminants. The buildup of unwanted contaminants can be controlled by (in order of decreasing effectiveness):
* keeping outdoor pollutants outside the house
* avoiding the use of pollutant-generating interior finishes and smoking
* isolating occupancy-generated pollutants in special rooms (bathrooms, kitchen, hobby, or workshop)
* filtering indoor air and diluting it with outside air through ventilation.

All four strategies must be combined to ensure good indoor air quality and humidity control. Even with careful selection of clean building products, continuous ventilation is essential to control occupant-generated odours, moisture and carbon dioxide.

Continuous ventilation is essential.

Heating Systems and Ventilation

From a ventilation perspective, there are only two types of heating system: forced warm air and all others.

The appropriate ventilation strategy is different for different house types, sizes, climates and choices of heating system. The decision about which system to use for heat should be made before the ventilation system is chosen. Both heating and ventilation systems should be selected before construction is started.

From a ventilation perspective, there are only two types of heating system: forced warm air and all others.

The heating system should be selected before the ventilation system is chosen; both should be chosen before construction is started.

9. Ventilation Systems

Ventilation with Forced Warm Air Heating Systems

In homes heated by forced warm air, fresh air may be distributed through the heating duct system. Fresh air can be drawn in from the outdoors directly into the return duct of the furnace or delivered to it by a heat recovery ventilator (HRV). If an HRV is used, fresh supply air is ducted from the ventilator to the return air side of the furnace. The furnace fan, running constantly on low speed, mixes this small quantity of fresh air with the large volume of room-temperature return air in the furnace ducts and filters both. The fresh air is delivered to each 'warm' air grille of the house.

Exhaust air is typically drawn directly from an exhaust grille placed high on the wall or ceiling of the kitchen and bathrooms. In good systems this operates continually.

Forced warm air heating system ducts, installed professionally, have generally been adequate for heat. However, when a heating system is used for the combined purpose of distributing ventilation air it will be run continuously at low speed. To ensure the system is quiet the heating ducts must be adequately sized so air noise is not generated. The exhaust portion of the ventilation system should also be sheet metal ducts.

When the same sheet metal ducts are used for ventilation purposes as for heating, the ducts will only be adequate if they are thoroughly sealed at all joints, elbows and splices with a duct sealant. Field tests have shown that often only 40-60% of the ventilation air system's capacity is drawn from where it is supposed to, the rest is lost to leakage in the ducts. This means that the effectiveness of the ventilation system is often poor.

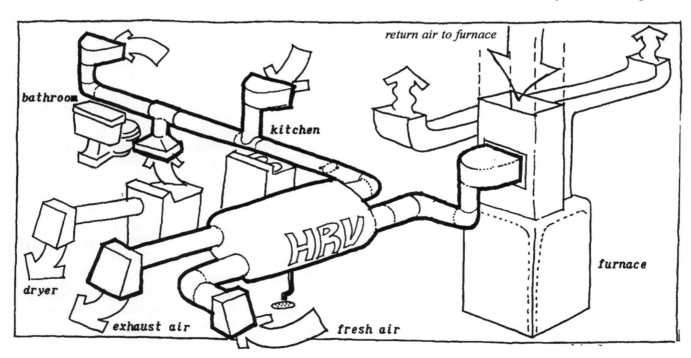

9. Ventilation Systems

Ventilation with Non-forced Warm Air Heating Systems

Homes heated by systems other than forced warm air, such as baseboard or radiant heating, are vulnerable to problems due to low air exchange rates.

In homes with forced warm air heating the furnace blower and ducts create zones of pressurization and depressurization increasing the air exchange with the outdoors whenever the furnace is running. This is a principal reason why forced air heated homes have historically not suffered the consequences of ventilation shortfall that non forced air heated houses have. The difference is magnified when electric baseboards are used because there is no continuous exhaust provided by passive chimney exhaust as happens with gas fired boilers and water heaters or wood burning fireplaces with poor fitting dampers (or none at all). In effect, the air loss up a warm undampered chimney will continue uninterrupted through the winter providing an air exchange for the house.

The lack of fresh air distribution contributes moisture and indoor air quality problems in many homes with non forced-warm air heating. That is why a house without forced warm air heating should be fitted with a fully distributed ventilation system.

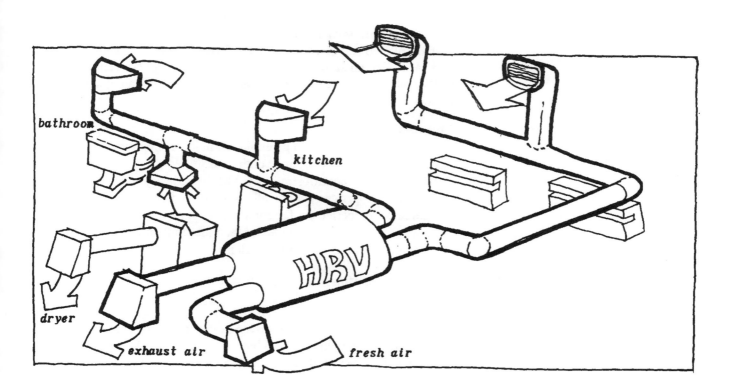

9. Ventilation Systems

Elements of a Ventilation System

All ventilation systems have three components: exhaust, fresh air, and controls.

Exhaust

Air has to be exhausted from the house. The most effective location for the exhaust grilles is at the ceiling in the kitchen and bathrooms, where the pollutants are skimmed off.

Fresh Air

Fresh air has to be introduced into the house. This can be done in three ways:

1. Passive inlets. These are specially designed vents that allow only a certain amount of outside air to enter a room directly. There are limitations on the use of this type of system. They are only suited for use in small to medium sized houses with non-forced warm air heated houses, with no cold chimneys, in moderate heating climates (with outdoor design temperatures no colder than about 0°F or -18°C). Unfortunately, there were a number of inappropriate applications of this system a few years ago, so some building codes do not permit their use even where they may be appropriate.

2. Fresh outdoor air delivered to or drawn into the furnace return air system, filtered and distributed by the furnace air circulation blower.

3. A dedicated supply fan, such as in a heat recovery ventilator (HRV) that draws and distributes the fresh air through an independent set of ducts.

Controls

Three means of controlling ventilation in increasing order of effectiveness: intermittent, interval, and continuous.

An intermittent control strategy is like the ordinary bathroom fan switch. It only operates periodically when turned on. Interval controls are programmed to operate the fan for a preset on and off time period throughout the day. These are better than intermittent controls, but not as good as a continuous ventilation system.

Types of Ventilation systems

Exhaust Ventilation

There are two basic exhaust driven systems: one uses isolated point-of-exhaust fans (i.e., kitchen and bathroom fans) and the second uses a central exhaust system. The fans may or may not be wired and controlled for the whole house.

The instant an exhaust fan is started, replacement air will enter the house. For this type of system to be truly effective, the intake and distribution of fresh air must be designed.

9. Ventilation Systems

A centrally located exhaust fan must be acoustically isolated when installed to be quiet. It must also be designed for continuous operation with automatic controls and manual override. Exhaust grilles for this ducted system must be located in the bathrooms and kitchen. The central exhaust fan should be located remote from living and bedroom areas to help ensure quiet operation. The finished installation complete with ducts, dampers, grilles, etc. will determine how much noise is developed.

Concerns are expressed that exhaust ventilation systems can cause spillage from susceptible combustion appliances. The air flows involved in a ventilation system are sufficiently modest that in most houses it is unlikely to create a problem. However, large capacity exhaust appliances, such as large kitchen fans (especially downdraft cooktops) are much more likely to create negative pressures big enough to be of concern, especially in tighter, draft-free houses.

Large capacity exhaust fans, such as large kitchen fans (especially downdraft cooktops) are likely to create negative pressures to be of concern if there are other combustion appliances in a home.

Supply Driven Ventilation

Supply driven ventilation systems push air into the house. Air exits either through deliberate openings or leakage paths in the building envelope. This is an appropriate system in hot, predominantly cooling climates. There is a concern, however, that with the better draft proofing of today's homes, the higher humidities in the homes in predominantly heating climates, the moist, warm air can be driven into the wall and attic to cause structural moisture problems. In extremely cold weather, window and door locks can freeze. The effectiveness of the ventilation is lower because there is no skimming of exhaust from the bathroom or kitchen ceilings.

Supply air systems are the most commonly used ventilation systems in homes with forced air heating in North America. A fresh air duct (often a 4" pipe) is connected from the outdoors to the furnace return air duct. Fresh air is then drawn into the house and circulated whenever the furnace blower is started. However, the amount of air drawn is variable - it may be large, or none at all, especially if the connection to the return air duct is at the end of the duct where there is little vacuum to suck outdoor air in.

The daily ventilation air intake volume depends on the operating time of the furnace. In cold weather when the ventilation need is lowest, the fan operation period is longest which can cause excessive dryness and wasted energy. In the spring and fall, when there is little call for heat, and a larger need for ventilation, there will be insufficient air exchange in the house.

Double Flow Ventilation

Double flow systems incorporate two independent fans. One exhausts stale air, and the other supplies fresh air to the house. It is the ability of this system to actively draw in fresh air and deliver it to the rooms where the occupants can feel it which makes this a useful system. A method of

9. Ventilation Systems

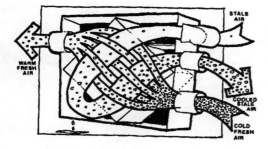

preheating or tempering supply air before it enters occupied spaces may be required. Heating and filtering the air is possible due to the presence of a supply fan for the fresh air.

Heat Recovery Systems

A heat recovery ventilator (HRV) is a packaged unit that incorporates air-to-air heat exchange. The function of the HRV is first to ventilate a home and secondly to temper the fresh replacement ventilation air. Heat recovered from exhaust air is used to temper the incoming cold air. This reduces the energy loss associated with ventilation, which can be valuable where heating fuel cost is high, the climate cold, and occupancy levels high, requiring high ventilation levels.

Air is exhausted continuously at a constant rate. Replacement fresh air is drawn in by a fan through a recovery mechanism that prewarms the air supplied to the house. Except for the higher installed cost, and the need to clean filters and inlet hood, double flow heat recovery ventilators have almost no liabilities. Like any constant flow exhaust systems, they do not really satisfy changing needs. However, with heat recovery a slightly higher base rate may be established without serious energy or comfort penalty.

In a non-forced air heating system, additional distribution ductwork for the supply air distribution is needed. In a forced air heating system the heating system ducts may be used for distribution of fresh air, and there is only a small added cost for the installation of a 2-speed furnace fan if the furnace does not have one.

Design Considerations

A home's ventilation design recognizes two groups of spaces: the main living spaces (living, dining, bedrooms, etc.) and service rooms (kitchen, bathrooms, utility). Areas such as hallways, storage rooms or mechanical spaces need not be ventilated directly as they are normally unoccupied spaces.

We need better air quality in the living spaces than in the service rooms. We can improve ventilation system effectiveness by supplying fresh outdoor air to all living rooms and exhausting stale air from the service rooms near the source of most pollution. This way pollutants are collected and removed nearer their source rather than being mixed and diluted through the house.

Our sense of fresh air quality is determined by what our nose "sees" and not what our feet "feel."

Our sense of fresh air quality is determined by the air our nose "sees" and not the air that our feet "feel." In most houses, the worst air (the air most in need of being exhausted) collects at the ceiling. In the kitchen and bathrooms, heat from cooking and bathing lifts the odours and moisture to the ceiling. In the living areas, body pollutants are lifted by the 100 watts of body heat we each generate. From a ventilation point of view, this stratification can help improve the effectiveness of ventilation if the exhaust grilles are placed near the ceiling because pollutants are maintained near the ceiling. In most homes, even if the heating system is forced warm air and its blower is running continuously, there is little to disturb this layering so exhaust from this level can really enhance ventilation effectiveness.

How Much Ventilation Do You Need (System capacity)

How much ventilation is required? We can only begin to set ventilation rates when we realize that we cannot count on opening a window to provide reliable ventilation, and once we realize that no amount of ventilation can ever do the impossible task of adequately diluting the ongoing emissions of unhealthy furnishings and interior building finishes. Confusion is increased because of the wide range of house sizes built today to accommodate one 'family'.

The ventilation system capacity must take into account two different ventilation needs - for spot ventilation and for continuous background ventilation.

Spot ventilation is the temporary exhaust all homes need during cooking and bathroom use. This is most effectively provided by ceiling mounted bathroom fans and updraft kitchen range hood fans. These exhaust fans typically may be used for 30 minutes per day (or 2% of the time per day).

Continuous background ventilation. We have now learned that ventilation is required for people, and that a continuous ventilation rate of 15 cfm per person is very effective at diluting the moisture, odour and carbon dioxide generated by individuals. Ventilation at these rates will also help dilute minor emissions from interior building finishes. Increasing these ventilation rates will provide only dimishing returns. Reduction of volatile organic compounds from materials in the home can only be provided by elimination or encapsulation of the contaminants.

Ventilation systems are evaluated in terms of how much air they can move. Total capacity must meet the desired objectives. However, the system need not run continuously at its maximum rate. A speed control for fans generally can only raise the maximum air volume to twice that of the low speed.

System capacity is measured in terms of total volume of air moved in cubic feet per minute (cfm) or litres per second (l/s).

System Controls

Ventilation systems can be controlled manually or automatically. Manual controls can be a standard on-off switch, a timer switch for each exhaust fan, or a switch at each exhaust point in a central system. Automatic controls can be a dehumidistat or time-of-day timers. Continuous operation is best, so a dehumidistat may be redundant.

Note that interior materials and furnishings, such as towels, clothing, bedding, upholstered furniture, carpets, textured ceilings, painted drywall, etc. have a great affinity to quickly absorb ("adsorb") odours

9. Ventilation Systems

and moisture, and also to release them over time. The adsorption time is short, but the discharge time is many times longer (10 to 100 times). These volatiles eventually release themselves from their hosts and re-enter the living air space. To control the buildup of the pollutants, a small constantly running exhaust will be more effective and energy efficient than a larger fan run intermittently.

Noise

A good ventilation system should not be heard.

Any noise generated by the ventilation system is an annoyance. An effective ventilation system should not be heard. If the system is loud, you will not use it as often as you should. If it is automatic and loud, you will try to disconnect it.

Some sound may be tolerable in a spot ventilation system, but a background air exchange system is only acceptable if it is quiet and transparent. The best, quietest fans will have a sound rating of 1.0 sones or less (as rated by the Home Ventilating Institute or HVI).

Maintenance

Yes

No

Most of us do not maintain our house as thoroughly as we should. The ease with which the maintenance can be done must be kept in mind when selecting a ventilation system. If not maintained properly, the best designed ventilation system will not do its job. However, as other elements in a home, all ventilation equipment needs maintenance. Good systems will be operated 8760 hours per year, or almost 50 times the number of hours a standard bathroom or kitchen fan may be run.

A continuously operating system will move from 4,000 to 12,000 pounds of air (30 to 120-cfm) each day, to and from the house. This means that equipment and grilles will collect dust and dirt that has to be cleaned from time to time.

Ensure that the placement of equipment allows easy access for service. The quality of service you as an owner receive is directly related to the working conditions for the service person. If equipment is located in a hard to reach attic or crawl space where only a midget Olympic gymnast can reach, it will not receive proper service and you will suffer.

HRVs have filters inside the unit that should be cleaned or replaced several times a year. Intake hoods on the outside of the house have ¼" bird and insect screens that accumulate debris and can plug up, so should be placed in an accessible location for a biannual inspection and cleaning. Motors have to be oiled periodically.

10. Air Filtration

Filters clean the air. They should not be confused with air circulation or ventilation.

Dust is everywhere in the home, always. The air we breathe is a mixture of atmospheric gases and dust particles. For good indoor air quality, the objective is a clean, odour free environment with low levels of particles.

House dust is made up of small particles generated by many different products that include fibres from clothing and furniture, floor coverings, pollens, animal dander, dirt, skin flakes, smoke particles, microscopic organisms (mould spores, mites and mite droppings and a variety of microbes). In other words, bits from any product that can wear down. (For example, the black oily smudge one gets in urban areas or near highways is vehicle exhaust and tire rubber worn off the passing traffic.)

House dust is made up of small pollens, bits from any product that can wear down and can include pollens, animal dander, skin flakes, smoke particles, and microscopic organisms.

Other sources of pollution are gases that may be either irritants or toxic, such as carbon monoxide, hydrogen sulphide, aromatic hydrocarbons and many others - a chemical soup of products found inside buildings. The source can be combustion (flue gas spillage), natural chemical reactions between products in the building, or the off gassing of products (the new home or new car smell is caused by the off gassing of chemicals as they set and age). The primary offenders in homes are floor coverings, paint finishes and cabinet particleboards. Fortunately the concentration of the chemical soup is often low. However, even in low concentrations, some combinations can be toxic if exposure continues over a long time as some people can become sensitized more quickly than the time it takes for finishes to become benign.

How to Clean the Air?

To ensure good air quality and clean the air indoors you want to be able to reduce the number of unwanted particles in the air. Filtration is essential to achieve this. Think of the filter as a strainer that picks out the offending particles. To be effective, the filtration must be able to do the job required. This demands a system that can move large quantities of air past good filters capable of removing the pollutants you want to eliminate.

The filter works like a strainer that picks out particles in the air.

This means that you must have some form of duct system to move the air in the house past the filter. This is easily accomplished with forced warm air heating systems, but not with non-forced air systems that don't have ducts.

Filtration is easily to do with forced warm air heating systems.

Contrary to popular belief, as the particles are filtered out and become trapped on the filter, the layer of accumulated particulates can actually make the filter more efficient. However, too big a buildup creates a resistance to air flow, lowering the amount of heat delivered. Eventually very little air flow goes through the filter, which then must be cleaned or replaced. This limits the filter life for furnaces, heat pumps and air-conditioning systems because such reductions of air flow increase operating costs and can cause accelerated wear on the equipment.

10. Air Filtration

What is an Efficient Filter?

You need to know what you are trying to filter, and how big the particles are.

It is important to realize that a 30% efficient filter could be much more useful than a 90% filter, as there are several test methods used to define filter efficiency. Each test is effective for a range of particle sizes to be filtered out.

You need to know what you are trying to filter, and how big the particles are. Think of it like the screens used by gravel pit operators - they have a range of meshes, each progressively finer, until one screen allows only sand to pass through. Within the limits of each size range, each screen is very efficient at holding back material of a given size. The same applies to filters.

The particles we are most concerned about are those capable of damaging the lungs. Through its respiratory system (nose, windpipe and lungs) our body can filter out particles larger than about 8 microns in diameter, and some down to about 3 microns, mostly through the lining in your nose and windpipe. (When you are in dusty environments, and sneeze and have to blow your nose often, your body's primary filters are cleaning themselves).

Our body cannot filter out particles smaller than 3 microns.

Your body cannot filter out particles smaller than about 3 microns so these particles enter your lungs, where they settle out on the lining. Once these particles are in the lung, over time some can eventually cause lung diseases or even death. In a polluted environment, the greatest number of particles will be smaller than 3 microns.

A standard throw-away furnace filter may remove all the particles larger than 5 microns in size. This could be expressed as an 80% removal rate (by weight). However, particles larger than 5 microns account for only 0.18% of the total number of particles in the air. (Larger particles may very well drop out of the air by gravity.)

Filter system effectiveness is based on a combination of filter efficiency and the volume of air (per hour) that passes through the filter.

How is Filter Efficiency Tested?

Filters are tested using one of three test scales.

Right now there are three test scales by which filters are tested. Test standards are being modified, so in the future all filter efficiency tests will refer to the effectiveness of filters for a given range of particle sizes. In order of increasing efficiency, the tests currently used are the Dust Arrestance Test, the Atmospheric Dust Spot Test and the DOP Test.

Usually, the smallest particle a human eye can see is around 10 microns in diameter (one millionth of a metre). The *Dust Arrestance Test* (ASHRAE Standard 52-76 Arrestance) measures how effective a filter is at removing particles of a specially prepared sample of air and dust. This is also known as the Arizona road dust test. It includes dust gathered in the Arizona desert plus powdered carbon black and cotton lint. This test is effective at measuring the filtration capacity for large particles (the smallest to about 5 microns).

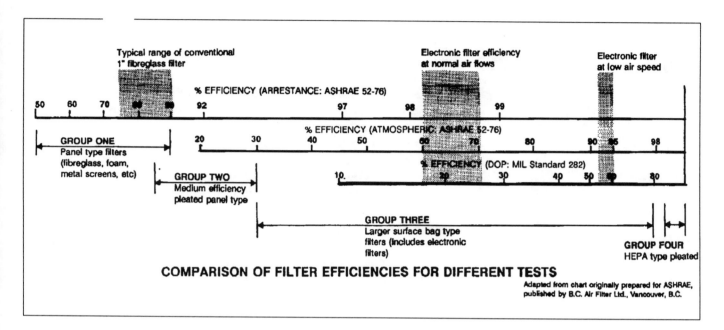

COMPARISON OF FILTER EFFICIENCIES FOR DIFFERENT TESTS

Adapted from chart originally prepared for ASHRAE,
published by B.C. Air Filter Ltd., Vancouver, B.C.

The *Atmospheric Dust Spot Test* (ASHRAE Standard 52-67 Atmospheric) can determine the effectiveness of filtration for particles as small as 2 microns. This represents the major portion of atmospheric dust and is the most common reference standard used today.

The *DOP Test* (MIL Standard 282) is effective at testing high efficiency filters designed to filter out particles in the 10 to 0.5 micron size range. This is the test used for the high efficiency particle arresting (or HEPA) filters.

Filter Types

Media Filters

Media filters are simple in their operation. Dirty air is drawn through a porous filter, and particles are trapped by the filter material while the smallest ones pass through. There are many types and shapes of media filters, ranging from regular furnace filters to units with an electric charge to attract particles more effectively.

Panel type filters may be made of spun glass fibres, open cell foam, expanded metal meshes, or woven synthetic fibre screens.

Common furnace filters primarily protect the furnace blower from large particles that might clogg the furnace fan. These filters (typical throw away or washable furnace filters) are cheap but are only 5-10% (arrestance) efficient at removing small particles in the air stream. They are good at filtering out large particles (as small as 10 microns) without restricting air flow - this is the reason that many people think forced air systems are dusty.

These inexpensive filters (around $1 per filter) should be replaced regularly to prevent reduction of airflow across the heating appliance. This type of filter is most commonly used as filters for furnaces and

Regular furnace filter is good mostly for larger particles.

10. Air Filtration

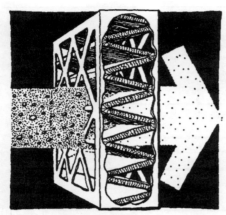

Medium efficiency filter is more effective for removal of smaller particles.

HRVs, where the main goal is to protect the equipment, not to clean the air. The washable, reusable foam or metal mesh filters are more expensive but do only a slightly better job.

Pleated panel type filters made of fine non-woven synthetic or synthetic-natural fibre are often called medium efficiency filters. Medium efficiency filters are perhaps the most cost effective means of reducing dust when installed with a continuously running forced air system. These filters may be up to 92% efficient ('arrestance') at removing particles more than 10 microns, and 30-50% efficient ('atmospheric') at removing particles down to about 5 microns.

Medium efficiency filters are efficient at removing larger particles, such as lint, pollen, and mould spores, and can remove particles as small as 1 micron. Tobacco smoke (50% particulate matter, 50% odour) is much smaller (in the 0.1 micron range), so only 5-15% of the smoke can be filtered out. Because medium efficiency filters are more dense, they must be replaced 2 or 3 times per year if they are not to reduce air flow.

At $10 - 18 (depending on size), medium efficiency filters are reasonably priced. They are not reusable, but depending on how dirty a location is, they may be good for up to one year. Because these filters may be deeper (2-4 inches or more) a special place must be made in the ducts to hold them. They come in the same sizes as many residential electronic filters. If your system has been prepared to receive an electronic filter, a medium efficiency pleated filter can be used in its place. For most applications, this is the best buy.

Extended surface or **bag type filters** have a larger surface area than pleated filters. They may be 24" deep or more, and are often called "bag filters." They are made of similar materials as the pleated panel filters but have a finer fibre mesh and are much more efficient. This range of filters can be up to 98% efficient ('atmospheric') at removing particles down to 5 microns, and up to 80% efficient (DOP) at removing particles as small as 0.3 microns.

Bag filters cost about $ 40 - 70, and require physical space and preparation of the ducts to provide a place for them, but in a typical home one filter may often last up to two years. This filter type is recommended when you want a clean environment.

Passive electrostatic filters, usually polypropylene fibres, become charged by the air flow through the filter, thus attracting dust particles in the air stream. Electrostatic filters require a constant air flow to maintain the charge that holds the dust. When the air flow stops, the electrostatic attraction is lost and the particles can be discharged back into the air. Unlike media filters, their effectiveness decreases when the air is humid. Once full, the air flow may push the dust back into the air stream because the charge is lost.

Electronic filters are more efficient, and are also the most expensive filters, with a typical price range of $650-700. Their high voltage and charged wires give a positive electrical charge to particles in the air stream as they enter the unit, then trapping them in a negatively-charged series of plates. Under some circumstances these may be more efficient than media filters. They require electricity to maintain their charge, and while effective, are very sensitive to the velocity of the air stream.

They can remove 70-90% dust spot (filtering particles as small as 0.01 microns). Electronic filters, however, can produce ozone (an irritant for the body) at very low air flows, and require regular cleaning to remain effective. Efficiency decreases as air flow increases and the collection plates become dirty. The filter becomes noisy as the electric charge zaps passing particles.

Electronic filters should have a low efficiency pre-filter upstream in the duct to capture larger particles that could short circuit the electronic charges, and to act as a distribution panel to help equalize the air flow through the electronic filter.

For maximum efficiency the unit has to be removed and cleaned frequently, as often as once a month. A more serious drawback is the ozone generated by the high voltage electric field used to charge the particles.

HEPA filters are the most efficient filters. HEPA filters are similar to the bag type filters, but they use ultra fine fibre fabrics. This class of filters is typically used for clean room applications - such as over hospital operating rooms, electronic clean rooms, etc. These filters can remove as much as 99.99% of all particulates 0.3 microns and larger.

HEPA filters require a special fan and filter holder because they are much bigger than a standard furnace filter (typically 24"x24"x12" to 24"). HEPA filters resist air flow more than standard furnace filters so the heating system has to be designed accordingly. The HEPA filter has a higher resistance to air flow so it has to be sealed at the edges to avoid air bypassing the filter. Because of the greater filter cost, it is a good idea to have lower efficiency pre-filters to capture larger particles out of the air stream before the air goes through the HEPA filter.

Turbulent Flow Precipitation (TFP) is a new filter technology that has been developed in Canada by Nutech Energy Systems Inc. In this filtration system small particles are trapped on the filter medium as the air stream passes through the filter unit. However, unlike other filters, the air stream does not actually go through the filter, so there is no pressure drop in the duct system. The TFP is very effective for filtering the small particles other filters do not.

Odour Control Filters

These filters use activated charcoal or other chemicals to remove odours and toxic gases. They are generally granules of the compound that absorbs the gases of concern.

Activated charcoal is the most commonly used filter medium. Charcoal is very efficient at adsorbing common smells. In areas subject to atmospheric inversions and where many people burn wood, charcoal is an effective filter for use on the intake in continuous ventilation systems to keep out smoke.

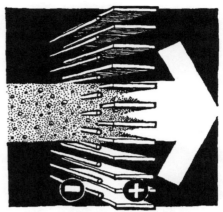

Electronic filter is effective for small particles, but requires regular maintenance.

10. Air Filtration

Recirculating range hoods rely on charcoal. Unfortunately, there is so little charcoal in these filters that unless they are recharged regularly (up to once a month if used frequently) they do not do anything.

Fortunately, the circumstances requiring these odour control filters are not often used in homes. They are normally used only in special situations, as they are expensive to buy and monitor and not always necessary. However, some chemically sensitive people find odour control filters beneficial. The nature of pollutants that are being filtered must be known to use the correct filter medium.

Filters and Heating Systems

Air filtration is a natural for houses with forced air heating systems, as good filters can easily be added to the ductwork. Airstream filtration is a good opportunity to reduce pollutant levels effectively. A convenient place to put these filters is in the return air duct, next to the furnace. To be effective, the furnace blower should run continuously: a two-speed motor should run continuously at low speed, switching to heating or cooling are required.

Filtration in Non Forced Air Heating Systems

An air handling system dedicated for air filtration must be used with non-forced air heating systems. In reality, this means having a fully ducted system throughout the house, with a blower unit and filter box. If a fully ducted ventilation system is desired, then the design could be modified to include filtration.

Good filters can easily be added to the forced warm air heating, but the furnace blower has to run continuously.

There are many sources for additional information, but few cover all aspects of heating systems in a general and comparative manner. Our list is not exhaustive, but provides some sources to pursue for more information.

Utilities

Utilities, especially the public utilities, have traditionally been a major source of reasonably unbiased information. Their customer service departments have a wealth of information that has been readily provided to customers. Because demand side management has been a significant strategy in energy supply, many utilities have also provided good information about other fuel sources and energy conservation options.

Unfortunately, with the deregulation movement today, new management approaches to customer service and decreased regulatory activity, the scope and reliability of utilities to provide unbiased information may decrease over time. As the utilities transform themselves into commercial marketing entities in a deregulated environment, there could be less incentive to provide a public service and be an arm of public policy. Rather, they could become more interested in marketing their product and retaining customers. (This has already happened in the USA in areas where deregulation has already occurred. The same scenario could be repeated in Canada, as, after all, what marketing organization can stay in business by telling a prospective customer that they really should use the competitor's product?)

Despite this, your local utilities are still a good source of information.

BC Hydro
BC Hydro customer service: phone 1-800-663-0431
www.bchydro.bc.ca

BC Gas
Customer Service Information phone 604-293-8888
www.bcgas.com

Enbridge Consumers Gas
enquiries:
Greater Toronto Area: 416 495-5504
All other areas: 1-800-314-5020
http://www.cgc.enbridge.com/

Union Gas
enquiries: 1-888-71-UNION (718-6466)
http://www.uniongas.com/

11. Resources

Trade and Professional Associations

ASHRAE, the American Society of Heating, Refrigerating and Air-Conditioning Engineers

An international technical organization focussing on heating, ventilation, air conditioning and refrigeration issues. They write many standards that set uniform methods of testing and rating equipment and establish design and installation practices for the heating industry. Chapters exist throughout the world.

Head office: 1791 Tullie Circle NE, Atlanta, GA 30329
http://www.ashrae.org/

HRAI, Heating, Refrigeration, Air Conditioning Institute

A Canadian organization that represents heating, ventilation and air conditioning industry manufacturers, wholesalers and contractors.

Tel. (905) 602-4700 or 1-800-267-2231
Fax: (905) 602-1197
www.hrai.ca

Heating Ventilation Cooling Institute (HVCI)

A British Columbia based organization for the heating, ventilation and air-conditioning suppliers and contractors. They provide industry training and certification (mainly for forced air and ventilation systems).

199 - 916 West Broadway, Vancouver BC V8A 4T7
Fax 604-414-0444
e-mail: hvci@thecentre.com

Residential Hot Water Heating Association

A British Columbia based organization for water heating, suppliers and contractors. They provide industry training and certification.

199 - 916 West Broadway, Vancouver BC V8A 4T7
Fax: 604-414-0100
e-mail: rhwha@thecentre.com

Canadian Home Builders' Association

The national association for Canada's home building industry. Local associations can be found in all parts of Canada. Check your phone directory, the CHBA web site at *www.chba.ca*, or call 1-613-230-3060

Other organizations

Local organizations, which may or may not be associated with national organizations, are valuable information sources. Ask local heating trades wholesalers for information.

11. Resources

Government Agencies

Provincial Ministries responsible for housing and energy issues are a good source for information. They often distribute national publications, and also focus on local concerns.

In the USA, state agencies and energy extension offices provide similar services.

Canada Mortgage & Housing Corporation

CMHC is Canada's national housing research agency. They publish a wide range of publications on housing technology. The Canadian Housing Information Centre (CHIC) is the arm that handles information distribution. Some information is posted on the Internet. For information and for a catalogue, telephone: 1-800-668-2642, Fax: (613) 748-4069.
www.cmhc-schl.gc.ca

Institute for Research in Construction (IRC) at the National Research Council

Canada's construction research technology centre. Since 1947, IRC has provided research, building code development, and materials evaluation services. This organization drafts the codes and standards that are the basis of local building regulations. For information telephone:
613-993-2463 or 1-800-672-7990; Fax: 1-613-952-7673
www.nrc.ca/irc/irccontents.html

Natural Resources Canada (NRCan)

The national ministry for energy issues has set up the Office of Energy Efficiency (OEE). They have many publications on energy appliances and energy efficiency. Tel.: 1-800-387-2000 (in the Ottawa area: 995-2943).
http://oee.nrcan.gc.ca/oee_e.cfm

DOE

The United States Department of Energy has a vast quantity of energy on their Internet site: *www.eren.doe.gov/*

Other web sites

REED

The Residential Energy Efficiency Database is an online information service that focuses on housing technology.
http://www.its-canada.com/reed/

Solstice

Solstice is the Internet information service of the Centre for Renewable Energy and Sustainable Technology (CREST). This US site focuses on sustainable energy and development information, but includes valuable building related information.
http://solstice.crest.org/index.shtml

Home Builder Magazine

On-line version of Home Builder Magazine (USA) is a good source for other links. This is one of the leading professional builder's magazines in the US.

http://www.builderonline.com/

On-line Information Centre
http://www.aec-info.com/homes/index.html

Books and Publications

ASHRAE Handbook of Fundamentals
Published by the American Society of Heating, Refrigerating and Air-Conditioning Engineers, this is the engineers' "bible" for heating systems engineering.

This Old House Heating, Ventilation, and Air Conditioning, by Richard Trethewy Little, Brown & Co. 1994

The Quiet Indoor Revolution by Seichi Konzo, Small Homes Council-Building Research Council, University of Illinois 1992

Residential Energy, Cost Savings & Comfort for Existing Buildings, by John Krigger Saturn Resource Management, Helena MT (sponsored by the US Department of Energy) 1996

Solplan Review, independent journal of energy conservation, building science and construction practice. Covers all aspects of residential and small building technology for new and retrofit construction. Six issues per year.

Solplan Review, p.o. box 86627, North Vancouver, B.C. V7L 4L2
e-mail: solplan@direct.ca